KICKING ABUSE IN THE ASS

KICKING

ABUSE

IN THE ASS

brutally
honest
A ∧ memoir

KIM O'HARA

Waterside Press

Printed in the United States of America

First Printing, 2018

ISBN-13: 978-1-947637-56-6 print edition
ISBN-13: 978-1-947637-57-3 ebook edition

Waterside Press
2055 Oxford Ave
Cardiff, CA 92007
www.waterside.com

Cover design by Rick Penn-Kraus
Cover illustration by Loulia Bolchakova

Gale —
Thank you for
your wise
guidance + love.

For anyone who survives abuse and has
the courage to get happy.
Really happy.

TABLE OF CONTENTS:

INTRODUCTION

Y ou have found a home here if you are coming to terms with sexual abuse.

If you haven't yet properly mourned a long lost life. This is not a searing tell-all book about who fingered me, or being fucked in a closet. It's also not the long drawn out story of the twisted promise of love to a young child in her bed that messed with her head for the rest of her life. It's about the lie, that the abuse didn't happen, that disguised itself in sex and love, and drug and alcohol addiction. It's about four decades of stolen happiness and my actions to gain it back in three short years. I had repressed the truth that I was a sexual abuse survivor to the point that I knew I was surviving but I did not know from what. I waged wars with the unknown inside and outside of me every day. Then one day I woke up and knew. I wasn't taking back the happiness. I was creating it for the first time. I was equal parts excited and terrified.

The writing exercises in this self-help memoir provide the writing-healing map I created to support my emergence as an abuse survivor through my deepest most painful ruminations. It is a self-realized framework that produced incredible results. I brought a few of these exercises to my writing workshops, dropped the focus on abuse, and simply asked people to write about their shame, their trauma, how the world saw them. Tears flowed. I got emails of gratitude. I tapped into unresolved pain for people but I knew I needed to access more people. A small group of ten was not enough. I had to write the book.

My book is a guide for any kind of abuse survivor to recover through writing. It does not replace twelve step programs or therapy. It is a strong companion to navigate the trickery and deceit of suppressed abuse memories and mourn the carnage along the way. Vet our shame, our self-loathing and rise like a phoenix from the ashes to a greater selves.

My shit hit the fan big time after a lifetime of thinking I had it all under control even with tremendous amounts of rage and chaos. I had no idea I had a secret. I just thought I was really misunderstood and edgy. I was tough, yeah, that's what I was. Don't fuck with me, motherfucker. You know that voice. I don't say that anymore. I feel it sometimes, when my edges still get bumped or a core wound gets rubbed, but I don't act on it. It's a blessing that I waited so long to recover from sexual abuse because it made me a natural expert on expulsing it through writing. I had the writing career, so I could apply it. That is how we are going to do this. You, Me. We are going to take a writing journey together to healing.

You don't have to be a writer to do the writing work in this book. You just need to have paper and pen, or computer, and willingness for a whole lifetime of suffering to be splayed out onto the paper. I urge my readers to have a notebook and a pen handy at all times for those incredible revelations that happen on bus stops and in the middle of the night.

The first step to anything is just that... the first step. Accepting that it is time to write about the abuse. You can buy the book, but push it aside and ignore it. I urge you to dive right in the day you buy it. I want you to get happy as soon as you can. The sunlight stream down on your face in a park with your children, and you feel the warmth for the first time in a way you never felt it before. To hear a loud laugh, look around, and realize, fuck, that was me. To discover you like wearing blue blazers, and high heels, and taking twenty minute naps in the middle of a work day because you damn deserve it to be the fullest you that you can be for all the fantastic loving people in your life. Does that sound like a fairy tale? Far from it. You are still pumping your gas, but you are not pissed off when you pull in.

I turned my life around by getting into the remembering of the abuse right away. I pushed it aside for 44 years. How long have you been in denial? Long enough to be out of time for any more misery. It's time for happiness.

Millions of people have suffered from some form of abuse be it mental or physical. Some cases are more extreme than others. The universal factor is if you are trapped inside the denial of your condition, or ashamed of your story, you keep it inside.

Chapters one through ten of the book unravel all the conditioning that was developed from the repression of the secret. You will cry big wet tears when you write. Sob in a profoundly gut-wrenching way. Be equally disquieted when you laugh out loud. You will find the freedom in the many emotions that emerge from writing through your darkest hour. Sometimes it won't even be writing. Just a pen clutched by a fist scribbling ugly black scrawl on notebook paper. Rip away.

For those of you in therapy, the addition of writing through the feelings that come up will accelerate your healing. My sexual abuse therapy sessions spanned two years, and I wrote in between the sessions. I don't know about you, but I didn't want to sit in therapy and talk in circles for the rest of my life. I would sometimes bring the writing that became this book, in pieces, and read it to my therapist. Choosing a good therapist is key, and bad therapy can do more damage than good. In my case, if you really want to avoid starting therapy, you can sleep with the person you don't hire and work out some of your shit that way. Not advised. When you do get serious about your recovery, and you find that therapist who can hold all the space for your sudden visions or memories, you can write along in this book. What comes out is yours to share, burn, save. Whatever you need to do. It is your sacred space to write and find your new voice.

Then there is the choice to tell others; ex –spouses, lovers, parents, children. You want to do it in a way that doesn't harm people. You were abused. You do not need to be an abuser. We can become abusers in some form if we are not cured because we were hurt. That's what we know. The more I healed my soul, God pointed me towards the people I love. I either told them about the abuse, or simply got well around them. People you love notice you changing. How can they not when you are radiating your unique original self for the first time?

We also have bodies that we have to reclaim. They were used for another person's pleasure, desire or anger, once, five times, a lifetime? Once is all it takes for damage. We take our bodies back. I was a sex and love addict for a very long time. It was kept at bay in the fidelity of two long-term marriages, but when the 2nd marriage was over, the shit got a little gnarly. If you are sleeping with your ob/gyn who is sending you videos of him masturbating in his office with the "door unlocked to add suspense," you probably have a low opinion of your body and what you deserve in a sexual partner.

My inner child was not just pissed off. She was seething and she had run the show for decades. We can find your inner child, and what is so fantastic is I don't go to "woo woo" depths with this angle of recovery. Yes, I explain my resistance to the inner child, but I was able through writing to become that adult that could parent her, and let her be a child again. It was key to my new happiness.

Typically in unraveling abuse, there is a lot of yelling, cursing and in my case, begging for the anxiety attacks to pass. It couldn't be any other way. To release the emotional gook on a cellular level is bad-ass messy. Be a bad ass. In a new glorious loving way.

What dies is the old abused you so the new beautiful you can shine.

Once we go through the writing prompts, you will cultivate your feminine side. The vulnerable woman can grow up and blossom, as well as the abused man. Desire to have a bigger life with a loving partner arrives. Big smiles when I kiss and hug my children. It's glorious.

The second half of the book-chapters eleven through twenty -uncover my gradual life changes as I peeled back the old skin of a silent sexual abuse victim. While not always chronological, I do bring the reader through my writing journey in the act of getting sober from drugs, alcohol and sex addiction, as well as finding mediation, spirituality and a God of my understanding. I learned how to do acts I had never been courageous enough before to do on my own like get my own apartment with my kids, and take jobs that served a gap, form my own company, and enlist business and life coaches to expand the visions of my life. I started to see that I desired a greater visibility after hiding in the shadows. I even fell madly in love. I slowed down my experiences and lived in the moment, not constantly looking over my shoulder to see who was coming to get me, trick me. I was less scared of what I was not doing for another's expectations.

I have amazing emotional freedom today by walking through my life and seeing so many incredible miracles. By no longer yelling at everyone I love senselessly but reaching out and loving, and sharing in a deep vulnerable way. It's about the deep longing and pain one feels just when they start to pick up the pieces. You can pick up the pieces, and what comes with recovery is a bigger life that offers more challenges, but now on a different playing field. Free of secrets and in your fullest talents. Wow. Sounds fantastic, right?

I am a survivor of incestuous sexual abuse but I am not a victim. I am a leader, a warrior and an intuitive. I am resilient and mentally healed for participation in life on a more soulful and grateful level. I want this all for you. As you read this book, you will slough away the painful dirty layers to expose the shinning bright light of yourself. You will gain permission to accomplish great feats and you will receive new tools to thrive. My hope is to help one person at a time be lifted from the shameful secret of sexual abuse. Then that one survivor will beckon another and another. They will pass this book to someone hurting more than them who has been sexually abused. We can collectively grow as women and men who can change the face of the world with our powerful healing. We have a calling greater than what we could have imagined because we have survived. We are the warriors, we are the kings, we are the queens, we are the leaders and change agents of the world and it is our responsibility to go out there and make that change happen.

CHAPTER ONE
WHEN WRITING ABOUT YOUR ABUSE
FEELS IMPOSSIBLE

My cat ate chapters ten and eleven of this book. It had been sitting in draft form for months unattended on my floor. He has anxiety issues but as I stared down at the mangled pages I knew what he was saying. *Get on with it already.*

What saved my book from the jaws of the cat and urged its completion was another coach. I was invited to his weekend event where he encouraged us to make a list of everything we are resisting. I couldn't even put "finishing my book" on the list. I had too much resistance. A voice in my head told me my focus should be on every other life objective BUT the book. It was just a story, poor me. Who cares.

That night on my return home, I took a wrong exit off the highway, and that was the coming to Jesus moment. A velocity of rage cracked open, and safe in the confines of my car, I screamed. Loud, haunting, intense guttural screams mixed with tears.

My clarity came at that moment, wet faced, at 80 mph on a darkened highway. I had to finish writing this book. As I pounded the steering wheel, I knew of only one barrier. Me.

Resistance is a bitch. Resistance will attempt to annihilate your sanity every time you start working through the exercises in this book. It will tell you that you are lying, you are creating stories that are not true, that everyone will hate you and writing doesn't solve problems. It will tell you to just get happy already like normal people and stop your whining. So here is what we do with the voice of resistance. Open your journal, note the voices of your resistance, and tell them to Fuck Off. You are in charge of your recovery now. If you stay true to the fact that the life you were living before you found this book is not even 1% near to the life you deeply desire, you can shut out those noises and join me. We are going to take a ride.

Here is your first Writing Exercise:

WRITING PROMPT:

Make a list of all the reasons why you can't write about your abuse using this book. These are your resistances. Understand them and know you will continue to battle them, yet they will calm down. They are pathetically weak when they smell defeat.

My whole adult life, everything I did was hard. Let me re-phrase that. I made it all very hard. Everything required a lot of will and many times anger to push it to that next level that often really led to behavior that either harmed me physically, crashed vehicles, smashed technological devices or left me essentially disliked as a leader. When you think you are dirty and not worth anything on this planet, you over compensate by being attracted to the noise all around you that affirms you are not worthy. If you can win, if you can try and show how hard it all is which is why you ended up with so little or not what your heart wants, you are safe in that space for one more day.

I had a self will that found me the father for my children, gave me the miracle of pregnancy and child birth, and kept me alive through addictions and crazy behavior. That will was built on survival, of white knuckles on the wheel. Built on a lie. Slowly letting go of that will opened my heart to the connection of self-love. God wants me to see that this "hard work" to get to these places of being, the state of motherhood, the state of being an alcoholic in recovery, opening up sexual trauma recovery, are now gifts and require daily maintenance of a spiritual life. I get to look back and say, what did

I not do when I couldn't see a bigger life, when I thought there was only one way? I didn't listen to my heart, and it could have continued like that forever yet the seed of desire to find my true self did an override on the lie. One random Tuesday night four years ago, my ego lost footing, just enough to dislodge the abuse secret from my subconscious and enter my unconscious in a dream, where it sat for a very brief moment until I woke up and knew the lie. I knew the secret. Oh shit. I started to write about it with clarity.

In my childhood, the lightness of life had been taken from me by the act and secret of abuse, the silence and the rigidity. It was what was not said that hurt me more than the act in many ways. My confused little girl grew to be an adult in a perpetual battle. Don't dare cross me. I will destroy you. A heat inside would rise, boil, and I would race to my journal to write page after page of rage-fueled words about what everyone else was doing to me. I was still trapped in the mind of a ten- year old little girl sent to her room to write about why she was so angry. I would beg God to kill my parents and then beg him to keep them alive. Then I would write about my escape into the stars, far from this planet, high above this place. At ten years old, I was not telling my true stories to anyone. I was sexually abused until I was ten, and then it stopped, plunging me into a great despair of loneliness, abandonment and rejection. It is incredibly lonely to hold the secrets of abuse. The repressed pain and denial eats you from the inside. It's as if it didn't happen, yet it profoundly did. That makes a little kid pretty pissed off.

In my teen years, I partied and took mind-altering substances so I would not feel anxious when the loneliness engulfed me. In my 20's and 30's, I ultimately drank and smoked pot to assuage unrest. I would be on movie sets in charge of 150 people and feel incredibly edgy and alone. I had no connection to the woman in my heart and my body. I would run from everyone because I felt so disconnected and write for hours by myself. I was the girl who wrote alone in a room, but yet was profoundly disconnected to the truth. I managed to write a few movies that had deep heart, but they were along the lines of reunion and the decades that were passing without still knowing yourself. My writings begged for my exposure but I wasn't ready. Then when I was with people, I would create a lot of drama and confusion, which to me was connection. Later when I was healing, I had to face I was still attracted to people who have unmanageable lives because it was what I was used to. Slowly through writing and sharing, I discovered I don't like people like that. I don't want to be that kind of person. Healing your lonely heart can come through many beautiful people in your path especially if you don't need to label them. I allow healing and trust. I am safe with me today.

You would think with telling you all this, and coming from a couple decades of working as a writer every day, I would have written about my sexual abuse a long time ago. Absolutely not. Incestuous sexual abuse was almost too surreal to consider. I wrote about everything else under the sun you could imagine, or I wrote characters that could have personalities that were derivatives of abusive pasts. My will was so strong, and my resistance was so great, I held myself back from writing my truths for far longer than I want for anyone else. I was a writer for twenty years and yet blocked off completely from my heart connection with self.

You do not have to be a writer to do the writing in this book. You will, though, need to have a journal. Buy two. Have one in your backpack, and one at home. If you can, splurge for a 3x5 little notebook for your pocketbook or back pocket. Once we open the stream of consciousness, there is an information super highway, and the revelations will come flying at you from all directions. We need to catch those on paper.

WRITING PROMPT:

It sounds trite, but put your name and the date in the journal. Commit to this is the first day of the beginning of the rest of your life.

The reason I have you getting the journal after you did the first writing prompt in this book is I don't want those resistant voices in the journal. I want them on a piece of paper somewhere else, in a box or a desk drawer. They are not allowed to play in this space.

You no longer need to have a lonely heart in your recovery from sexual abuse trauma. I hear you. I see you. I am here to support your dream of truth. I know you won't judge me, my stories, as I won't judge you. If I can be without shame and whole, so can you.

WRITING PROMPT:

Who do you think will judge your abuse story if you tell it? What part of you runs the show?

You will tell your abuse story, it's cathartic to do so, but the actual story is not the abuse itself. It is what you are hiding behind, and what you are ashamed of. You need to dig it out and live with it for a little while. It hurts like hell, but on the other side of pain is profound healing. To no longer have any more secrets is to finally be alive.

Chapter Two
Remembering the Abuse
for the First Time

One morning at forty-four years old, I awoke from a very subtle dream and knew I had been abused. No validation was necessary. It was the truth. I had quit smoking pot a year prior, and my brain, literally reshaping and changing, had allowed acknowledgement to grow more powerful than denial. That distinct feeling of my dad in bed with me as a little girl, breathing on me, launched my recovery from incestuous sexual abuse. The timing of your discovery will be your own but chances are you have picked up this book since you know you were treated in an abusive way. Denial is what the ego uses to protect you, yet hindering you at the same time from healing and expansion. I have watched people's faces when they hear me speak about uncovering the truth about sexual abuse. They harden and shift. Then they come to me after, breathless with their confessions: "I gave him sex to get some candy. I thought that I was the bad girl." "My mother masturbated me for ten years and I thought I invited it." "If I told, they would kill him, and I wouldn't have a father any more."

My first knowing of the abuse was visceral. When I woke from that dream, I could recount vividly my father's feet approaching my bedroom door, the light blocked under the door crack, the door knob turning, his breath on me. I wish I could recall my exact feelings, but I know I was a scared little girl. So scared I didn't tell anyone for 44 years. Including myself.

WRITING PROMPT:

When did you know you were sexually or emotionally abused? Are you still fighting it? Write about that first thought or memory that made you sit up in your seat, gasp, wake from sleep, or freeze in the middle of a crowded store. Write about it regardless of your doubt to its truths.

The day after the initial dream, I called the couples' therapist who could not save my second marriage. I didn't know where else to turn and she had way of talking to me in the sessions that indicated she had a deeper view of my anger.

"I was abused," I sobbed into the phone to her. "I need help. Can I come see you? Can you help me?"

After consoling me, she told me she had a wonderful referral.

Then, and I can't explain why, I called my ex-husband. He was the key person who I had lived with the last decade of denial. It felt important he know. It was my first tiny step to recovery from the sheath of shame.

"I was abused," I said, tears streaming down my face.

"Oh … " he responded. "That explains everything."

I didn't talk to him about it after that.

WRITING PROMPT:

Who was the first person you told you were abused? Have you told anyone yet? Write about how it would feel or felt to "confess."

DID YOU BUY A JOURNAL?

This writing work deserves better than a random piece of paper you found in your kids craft drawer, or the back of a napkin. Honor yourself. Treat yourself. Buy a journal.

I had been tipped off to the abuse twice in prior years. The first time was when I was twenty-one years old and partying with my first husband, my dad, and one of his girlfriends at his country club. My dad was definitely an alcoholic but as the concept of AA was so far out of my sphere of understanding at the time, I identified him as my hard-partying forty-seven year old dad. (He would die thirteen years later in a third heart attack on my sister's couch.) Drinking with my dad, and the money he spent at the bar felt like fraternal love. At one point, I went to the bathroom and his girlfriend followed me. We were both pretty wasted. Before she went into the stall, she leered at me and asked, "Did your dad ever sexually abuse you?"

The wind was knocked out of me. It was such a bizarre question. I tried to think through the thick pall of alcohol but I couldn't come up with a response. Fuck no, my ego said, we won't believe it.

We silently peed and then when we washed our hands, I addressed her question with a question.

"Why did you ask me that?"

"Because he told me he did," she said, drunkenly smug, drying her hands.

I leaned against the cool tile wall of the bathroom, strained nonchalance.

"That's ridiculous," I said.

She stared at me with apathy.

"Really?" she said.

"Really!" I replied. "He's a drunk talking crap."

"Okay," she said. "It's your life." That was the end of it.

I felt sick to my stomach so I stuffed it down. Erased it out. Denial and acknowledgement had been in the ring, like a cage fight, and denial, without any bleeding, had won. We went back to drinking at the bar until last call. I even drove my drunken dad and his girlfriend home, a foggy sense in my brain, like a surreal hell, as they laughed in the backseat. It played again and again in my head as I tried to get my dad to give us directions back to his house. This was way before cell phones or GPS systems.

Did he abuse you?

I think I may have even put my dad to bed that night. Fucking drunken idiot.

I buried that conversation down so damn deep. I made sure it would never ever resurface. I told no one. I don't think I even told my first husband, or if I did, I told him as if it was a joke and that woman was a crazy drunk. I locked that shit away for twenty years. I never even thought about it again. Denial is such a powerful tool for survival. Denial wins if you are not ready. Little did I know not telling was going to make my life get gradually, slowly, a little uglier, a little messier and a little more addictive every year. I carried a heavier and heavier burden every single day. The secret of my sexual abuse ruled my behavior for four decades. I get today to tell this story to anyone in denial, and urge them to face the truth. Don't burn out half a life.

Two years ago a man approached me after I shared my story of facing my incestuous abuse. He sadly explained he had been abused but couldn't tell his mom. Until he heard me share, he had not had the courage to say it out loud to anyone. Especially not his parents. He was in his forties like me. I told him he had another whole half a life to go. I urged him to address the secret. He thanked me. I prayed for his healing.

WRITING PROMPT:

Where did you have deep denial versus acknowledgement of the abuse in your life? Do you feel like you have lost time? Take one dynamic that occurred in your life, divorce, job loss, a conflict with a friend, and play out where repressed abuse could have played a part.

My dad and I would continue our partying relationship through my late twenties and early thirties. While there was no longer abuse, I always felt self-consciously awkward around him. I purposely didn't wear any kind of revealing or overtly feminine clothing. It was like we were some broken up couple now just existing as friends. There was something about him that pervaded me, and my body had an edge of lack of safety when I was in his company. I understand now what I couldn't identify then … he made my skin crawl. Today, I apply that intuitive sensation to evaluate the safety of people. When I land in situations with people who are erratic, addictive, abusive, it only takes me three weeks to walk away versus forty years. Sometimes that hour on a day I am sharply attuned to my inner self. I was locked into an obligation to have my dad keep visiting me and visiting my dad. The abuse held us together like a tether. Now I live in an untethered life. I can love you, but I understand I can stand on my own.

My dad also sabotaged both my weddings. I have no idea if it was a subconscious sabotage related to the loss of the abusive relations, but at the first wedding he got ridiculously drunk at the rehearsal dinner. My maid of honor and I had to put him to bed. He was an embarrassment so I did what any good New Englander would do. Laughed it off. He walked me down the aisle hung over with one contact lens. This was the kind of treatment I learned to expect from a man, taught by the primary man in my life. Low life crap. Dishonor. Real shit. I never got that 'before the wedding daddy-daughter conversation', that 'I'm giving you away on your wedding day' love. I got a dad with a wicked headache, vomiting in the toilet and chasing his ex-wife around the after-party. I smiled like a brave girl through the whole big charade. The party must go on. The lie deepened. It was a mascarade.

He died a month before my second wedding so he ruined my glory by his untimely demise. Grieving is a complicated state especially when you don't have any idea that you are grieving the death of the co-conspirator of your maligned life. I was left alone with the lie. I learned a decade later he remained in my cellular nervous system, the abuse pattern, the imprinting, until I released him in recovery. He died but his abuse of me held me prisoner for twelve years after his death.

The second time I had a very vague hunch about the abuse was in my thirties.

My dad had impulsively moved to California after spending his whole life in Rhode Island. He showed up with a sparse collection of possessions recklessly tossed into the back of a leased Grand Cherokee. I figured he was here to clock in some grandpa time as his first granddaughter was a mere eight months. Like any new mother with limited help, I was eager to hand him the baby and run an errand. In the middle of the mall, a panicked feeling overcame me. I knew something was gravely wrong and I had to get home immediately. I drove wildly and burst into the house to find him with my daughter on the changing table playing airplane with one of the stuffed animals. I felt immediate relief, like I had just saved my daughter, although I had no conscious idea from what. I snatched her up and made the decision he would never babysit her again. I am confident nothing happened to her that day ... but if he had not died a week later, the abuse may have gone into the next generation. I may have had a change of heart and let him babysit. I may not have gotten that intuitive hit. I still did not allow a single thought of my abuse to come up from this stand alone incident.

I would be lying if I said I was sad when my dad died. Not right away. When I did mourn it was in a way that was forced and angry and confused. I smoked a lot more pot, drank more, and planned to have a second baby. Gotta keep moving no matter what.

WRITING PROMPT:

Is your abuser still alive? Have you had a chance to confront them? If not, or if it is not safe or wise to do so, write about what that experience would be like. Get as violent or fantastical as you would like. This is your repressed anger, your violation ... let it go on the page.

In the first year of facing the abuse, I wanted someone to appear that informed me I was delusional. It felt too horrific to accept. Yet I couldn't stop talking about it and no one stopped the chatter. Since the specifics of my abuse are incest, it felt more dirty and shameful than any other kind of abuse in my mind. Doubts whether the abuse memories were real cropped up as a defense mechanism against getting better. A wise person said to me when I voiced my doubt, "People generally don't use sexually abuse for popularity. So why would you do it?" Their confidence helped me push forward into the further depths of remembering. I discarded all theories of doubt. Every time I shared it out loud, the shame had a tiny bit less power over me. I was abused and I lived a painful life of isolation, aggression, lack of compassion, workaholism, lack of trust and addiction due to lying about it to myself. In order to face the truth in therapy, I had to be of one opinion. I was abused. End of discussion. My father, one of my primary caretakers, had breached and violated his bond to me as a child. Trust was shattered and contorted so I had lived an emotionally vague existence with people who thought they were close to me. I was a master of disguise, and I was a lot of fun. I knew as I recovered, I would start to have deeper relationships, but that involved a reshaping of my motives and my operating system. I would have to start trusting people.

Sexual abuse from infancy had developed primal fears that sabotaged the development of my whole true essence. It would come down to first learning that I wasn't such a bad girl. I had a right to all the good in this world. Taking my seat was one of the hardest tasks to unfold after the acceptance of abuse. I felt like an imposter but I was a survivor. No more lies for me.

I was not fabricating this "ailment" to justify why I was an alcoholic, why I had failed at getting to the top of careers I killed myself to achieve, why I could rage on my little kids. Sexual abuse contributed heavily to it, and now I had the task to get well and stop all the behavior that kept me from loving myself, and those who loved me. Future failures would no longer be blamed on this one earth-shattering psyche-changing trust-bursting neurologically shifting disassociating breach. I looked forward to that day.

I became a student on the subject of recovery. Most books guided me to be a survivor of sexual abuse, but not how to thrive in the history of sexual abuse. The writing felt archaic. Two prominent books were published over twenty years ago and geared to teach awareness of abuse so I would be on guard for the emergence of self-destruction. Facing fighter self was part of the journey, but I did not want to invite her to stick around. She needed serious help to cope with the truth, but what about real living? The books gave instructions on handling a flashback, or a stressful situation that mirrored the vulnerability of abuse, or how to talk to a partner about my sexual abuse. I flipped forward for the chapters on thriving and living a beautiful life but there were no such writings. Sure there is irreparable damage but there are assets to our trials. Where is the instruction booklet on what to do when I no longer wanted to die!!

I appreciate those books to hold me up in my early recovery, but I wanted more than tools for protection of my damage. As my self-love grew, and I started to shed the shameful actions of an abused mentality, I sought literature on thriving and empowerment after abuse. The more I came out of my shell and started to meet with and talk to amazing women, and coaches and entrepreneurs spreading their wings and achieving greatness despite abusive background, the urgency to write a sexual abuse book on letting out the self-lies and achieving success increased. It was a pounding insistence I would not ignore.

I learned about all kinds of abuse in my recovery research. Some people are emotionally abused. It doesn't matter what form the abuse is. It all erodes the soul center so you can't tap into your sensuality and freedom to be an adult. Then you go out with this low worth of self, and you attract narcissists that will continue to destroy you slowly. There is emotional incest where a parent makes the child their "surrogate partner" and divulges details of their problems with the other parents emotionally and sexually on an adult level with the child. This happens with mothers and their sons, and fathers and daughters, but I have also heard a lot of pain from men who were made "wives" of their fathers. One man I dated went everywhere with his dad as his constant companion. The dad hardly took the mom anywhere. The man grew up to be a very rigid controlling man. His healthy little boy identities were altered and twisted.

Neglect is abuse. Children grow up with low-self worth. They parented themselves at a young age because their parents were addicts or mentally ill. Children who were slapped when they cried and told never to cry again in public were abused. Silencing someone is abuse. These children went inside themselves, into the darkness with all their feelings.

Whatever the specifics are of your abuse, whatever age, race or gender, if you suspect it happened, I am going to tell you it did, for you. If you believe it, if there is a knowing in your heart, you can take it from me ... it is not some sick side of you trying to get attention. We don't go around talking about being abused. It's not cocktail party conversation. I was surprised in the midst of the final edit of this book, I doubted its validity again. What if I had made all this up? I called a close friend.

"What if it isn't true?" I said. "I want to just throw my whole book away."

I had gotten trapped in that web of guilt. My dad was dead and couldn't defend himself if this was all a sham. It was that old abuser hook. Don't tell anyone. This is just our secret. You love me, right?

She took not even half a pause before she said, "What's not true? That your father molested you?"

I had barely gotten a tentative "Yes" out of my throat when she said, "Oh honey, you know it's true. It's an absolute truth." She almost laughed. She had known many intimate parts of my recovery the last couple years. If anyone heard me in my most raw and vulnerable moments, it was this confidant.

"I know," I said. "And I have to finish the book because it can heal lots of people."

"What if the book leads to something good?" she said.

I got chills thinking about her response. It was spot on. What if good did come from this? How could there be anything worse than what I was writing about that already happened?

WRITING PROMPT:

Did you have a special bond with your abuser? If he or she was a parent, describe the special feelings about the bond despite the shame of it being connected to the abuse. Do you feel guilt about it? If not a parent, do you feel guilt in telling their secret?

With the writing prompts in this book, I know I am asking you to get really raw. Stay in the belief it happened, no matter what, and more will be revealed about the true essence of you as you write. While you are seeking to find that hidden person who has not yet grown out of the frightened confused child, you are ultimately looking for the good in all this. It is there. It can be found.

Chapter Three
Finding your New Voice

It's not okay that you were abused. You got that? Let that statement sit with you for a moment. It sounds obvious, right? Of course it's not okay, but think about how you feel when you read that out loud. Do you think for even half a millisecond you caused it? Throw that thought out the window right now. Stamp on it. Crush it. Never consider it again. Don't let anyone indicate or insinuate you did it. You did nothing. You were abused and you are reading this book because of it. Say a quick "Fuck You," get it out of your system and realign. We have some good work to do, and we don't need that shitty belief system hanging over our heads.

Okay, I wish it were that easy. That voice is in your head telling you in some way you either brought it on, or you are delusional about it, is strong and persistent! You still want to crawl into a hole and die. Repression of abuse does not go away overnight and the voices in our head are products of that repression. My ego wants me to be the same as I have always been because that's how it knows me. Now I am looking to shine and have a bigger life, and go after dreams in a new authentic self and my ego is freaking the fuck out.

It's not okay to have been abused. Say it a million times until you actually own it. You never have to be okay with it.

As survivors of abuse, we need to say it with clarity. Moving on is knowing, not being scared of it and then having a beautiful life despite it. It is also a process that happens over years depending on how deeply you want to vet it. Some days I'm really pissed. It sucks. It was wrong and I was victimized. People, adults, you trusted who should have shown you the world was safe and good as a child blurred it for you and darkened it and then threw you out to have to cope like an adult in a sea of other adults who had never been abused. Threw you into a sea of lucky people. I thought I was not lucky. It has nothing to do with luck. People do shit to people. My power is greater than that. No one action, even sexual abuse, can affect the role I can play in this world, in my life. I know that now. I am so grateful I do. It took me a whole three years of writing this book to find it. I hope for you that you can write about it sooner. I didn't have a coach. I had lots of writing resistance. We can change our stories faster and get out there and live our lives sooner. So I am a little bit of a cautionary tale.

Write soon and write fast.

My not telling anyone created doubt about my inner voice. If it said truths about the abuse, I felt it was madness so I smoked lots of pot to keep the voices away. At first how vivid it all was pained me, but now I've let it pass. It is no easy gig to come to the conclusion you have to hear the voice that's your voice at least once to face the truth; you were abused and violated. When you do, so many patterns in your life of rage, abuse, running, failed relationships, self-loathing, mutilation, addictions, under-earning, lying, stealing, infidelity, bulimia, weight gain, face picking, depression, just to name a few – can point to the one source that was shattered for you from the start. The life story you could have had until you were derailed by abuse.

I know sometimes you don't understand why you are screaming, and the people you are screaming at don't understand too. If you have not faced your sexual abuse, everyone in your life is an ignorant party. What a hapless way to live! Blocked from love. The yelling voice is the only voice that gives you power because your true self has been repressed and silenced. Development ceased at the first violation. You have been screaming at people for so long, in this justified rage and anger, you are tired. You have a shred of you that believes perhaps you aren't an angry person, just something happened to you that you can't quite put your finger on, that may have made you this angry. You have a glimmer from time to time that you are good, lovely, you go out of your way for your spouse, your kids, your friends. You are intelligent, productive and well-mannered. You have a good sense of style and you have shiny hair. You washed your car spot-free and you flew on a dream holiday to Maui. But still… there are the dark voices. The voices have taken your unshaped true self voice and darkened it to that tell you not to expect to be anything special like those "normal people". Why should YOU expect to have a greatness others have… the voice is sinister as it tells you that you are different. One day you will discover you are different but in a very magnificent way. You are a warrior. You will have a sword. You will use it in a strong way with love. You won't cut people down anymore because of your pain.

WRITING PROMPT:

What do the voices that you hear in your head tell you about yourself? I am particularly interested in the dialogue between the good voices and the bad voices. Write a scene where you give form and shape to the voices and see what kind of conversation transpires.

It is an understatement to say the revelation that you have been sexually abused is devastating. I am not discounting the process of realizing this fact at any age, but for me, facing it mid-life has created an enormous upheaval because it has forced me to question how I operated for the last 47 years and face the daunting task to be my full authentic self. I have to open myself up to spiritually hear only one voice, and that is the voice of a higher power. I recalled when I started to say "No" with my recovered voice and it was because I finally had choices. I heard me speaking, a "me" I had never met before and I was astounded. Hi "me," whoever you are.

It was not okay to be sexually abused and we need to use our voice to talk about that first and foremost. The rest of the world can wait. My world waited to begin until three years ago when I said "Yes" to accepting the truth and squashing the denial.

WRITING PROMPT:

How has your voice sounded different in recovery? Where did you stop and say, "I said that?" Write about a moment you spoke up and heard your voice in a new way.

Many times in my life when I have endeavored to do anything that took risk or belief in my intuitive drive, that sinister voice would chime in. I would will my way out of it but it had ultimate control of me. As I sat down to write this book, before my butt even hit the chair the voice would say, "You're fat. Who do you think you are sitting down to write a book that isn't even going to amount to anything or mean anything to anyone when you really should be working on making yourself more beautiful. You need to be more beautiful for anyone to love you. Isn't that how it's always worked?" I laughed at the voice. I confronted it. I said, "Wow! Seriously?" Or the voice tells me, "You have crappy clothes and no self image. You are poor and frumpy."

Astonishing that voice. Demonizing. It distracts me from my goal. It doesn't want me to get well and doesn't want me to help others. It wants me to be distracted by my dusty desk, or my meowing cat. It wants me to misconstrue something my boyfriend said so I can go into a three-day emotional bender, and then a two-day emotional hangover. The voices demand I listen to them. I don't want to listen to them anymore. They are extensions of me, and I am still fractured. I need to listen to my heart, not the voices. My heart as it heals knows what is best. When I listen to my heart, I can smile. I can write. I can breathe. I can love. I don't hear voices of any kind. A life without voices? Wow. A novel concept.

My sexual abuse at such a young age dictated so much of what I said and did for almost four decades. I have heard women share in twelve step meetings that because they were taken advantage of at a young age, because they complied, they operated on the assumption that they were promiscuous. They spent a lifetime giving themselves and their souls away sexually. That was their story and the voices confirm it. "Slut," the voices said. They now understand there is a chance they may not be promiscuous but rather taken advantage of by an adult that should have known better and altered their self persona forever. They may have a completely unformed and uniquely different sexual voice. It's human and sensuous to use your sexual voice free from abuse!

I learned while alcoholism or addictions are a spiritual malady, so is being sexually abused. Your inner spirit, your soul, has been punctured. If you are reading this book, then it is safe to say you, or someone you love, endured sexual, emotional or physical abuse as a child. So I am going to say this to you again clearly as I had to hear it a lot of times...

You did not cause sexual abuse, or any abuse of any kind.

There is the shame that somehow we brought on sexual abuse. Worse still, that we liked it! The voices, when they knew I was getting better, did a real shift one day to this concept. It staggered me emotionally for at least a week. What if I liked it? It was a super gross yuck, but luckily I had a therapist who made sure I knew that as a young girl, getting affection from my father was a natural yearning. How was I to know he took it too far? Who was I comparing it with? It's not like I went to school in second grade and said to one of my peers, "So, is it normal for your father to stroke you all over when you are naked?"

If it wasn't bad enough that I had endured a lifetime of a damaged and misaligned soul dying slowly underneath all the dark shame, now I got to loathe myself in a new way. I got to loathe myself in sexual abuse awareness. The voices that told me shameful things about myself now had a purpose, a cause. "I am a dirty shameful creature," I have heard beautiful women say at AA meetings. "I disgust myself. I was sexually abused, and I know it probably plays a part, but I just hate myself." Probably? Probably! I can assure you it plays more than a part. I took it lightly for a long time. But when I really knew, and when I realized that it no longer had to rule my life, when I knew I could take my voice back, I had to take action. Your calling is when your calling is. No one can rush that for you. It is a very painful and scary thing. There are a lot of stages you will go through with it, but I can assure you every stage is worth it. If you work it out on a man you are dating, and the relationship breaks up, it is not because you are a dirty, damaged sexual abuse survivor. It is because your voice was at the level of recovery it was capable at that time, and that man chose you to work out something in his own psyche. He was only able to express what his voice had evolved to in that space of time. He gave you the gift of the space and time to work out a piece of your abuse. If the relationship ends, move on. It's ok.

It's not worth it to hold it all inside. Those voices, they will kill you. You have to take action always moving forward in recovery, even if it means leaving some tread marks behind.

Sometimes in early recovery, there were no succinct words in writing. I would just take a pen and a notebook and allow my hand to angrily scribble. I would rip that paper to shreds with dark scrawling uncontrolled scratches, like I was possessed. I would do it with tears pouring down my face and dropping into the black slashes, making them muddied and even messier. Sometimes I would write with my nondominant hand and allow it to produce words like Ouch and Pain and Daddy and Hate and Fuck. Sometimes I couldn't read it at all and I didn't care. I would rip the garbled word vomits out of the notebook, ball them up and throw them across the room and then retrieve them and push them deep into the bottom of the trash. Then I would sit with my arms wrapped around my knees and shake. While those experiences were exhausting and frightening, I knew I was coming alive. The real me was taking flight.

I would sometimes write with such an urgency, desire and anger I could never read what I wrote but it got out a little more of that angry little girl voice inside who had to write perfect, "I'm sorry for my behavior" notes to her clueless mother. Silenced by another level of denial. It's a family affair.

WRITING PROMPT:

Can you let yourself go on paper without any need for it to be anything and see what can be set free? Can you scribble and just write words and letters? If you have to, just scribble wildly with a black pen on white paper. I did that many times with a clenched red face. It is releasing old toxic repressed energy in your body so new happy can come in.

Yes, we can start to control the voices.

Maybe you don't want to hear that.

You want to be an abuse victim for the rest of your life.

That identification is important to you.

This book does not take away that choice.

Sure I get scared, I am human, but I can walk through it knowing I am not unlucky, or marred or damaged. I am just in the course of this life.

The day I started to talk about my sexual abuse, I talked about it a lot and didn't care how long I was going to talk about it. First I was like, am I going to be that girl that has an abused identity? Then I realized it had always been my identity but the difference was … I lied about it. Now I was going to talk about it. No more lies.

CHAPTER FOUR
BATTLING ANXIETY ATTACKS/
GAINING SPIRITUAL PURPOSE

The anxiety attacks I experienced right before I faced the truth about sexual abuse, and through my recovery, were the most terrifying, debilitating incarnations of near death of my lifetime. Today I can manage them, but they are my little indicators, my inner spirit standing up inside, warning me I am not standing in my truth in any given situation, and should take serious notice. The anxiety attacks began initially in 2012 when I quit smoking pot and that cleared the neural pathways of my brain. New pistons were firing every minute that had once been dulled by big hits of pot. The small attacks became long ones. I would have the worst ones while I was working at Trader Joes. This job was part of my ground zero, my spiritual reboot. It's rigor and simplicity set the stage for me to face the abuse as I had the dream right before I started working there. Trader Joes provided a safe place to retreat during my second divorce and a career meltdown. For eight hours a day, people only knew me as Kim the Clerk. I would get the horrendous anxiety attacks while working the cash register at some of our busiest hours. Full exposure of self. I had to grab a buddy to cover the register so I could just die in the bathroom, begging God with tears streaming down my face to make it stop.

After I faced the abuse for a year, I stopped drinking for clarity about my new life. The attacks kicked up to a new level of obnoxious.

I thought, seriously? Here I am trying to clean out and come to terms with some pretty crazy shit and my body was doing whatever it could to make me say, Fuck it. This isn't worth it. I'll just go back to denial. Hand me some pot and a drink, please.

I didn't let my ego win. I hadn't gone this far to fall back.

I thought a few of those anxiety attacks that went on for an hour were going to truly kill me. They were debilitating. Bone crushing. The attack rips through you a bit at a time and you pray as your teeth ache sharply that your heart won't go into full arrest. My heart felt like it was being shredded and I would pray that it would hold up. I imagined only a small shard of my heart left to beat. I was transported to that same precipice as a small child being violated by a grown man who was my dear daddy. My throat would ache like nobody's business, raw and hot. Instruction from other abused women to stretch my throat and scream into a pillow didn't prevail upon these whoppers. Underwater bathtub screaming would not derail their descent.

One day, in the midst of one, I started to pray and was transported back to my little girl body waiting for the abuse to happen. The feelings causing my adult anxiety were distinctly hers. Would it be tonight? The childhood bed was big and wide and long and I almost didn't feel like my body was in it or I was a ghost of myself there. When my dad opened that bedroom door, I would leave my body and observe. Reliving that experience as an adult gave me a weird sensation across my cheek bones, the skin and blood underneath got cold like they were kissed by dry ice. Later when I wrote down my experience, my jaw locked and I felt punched in my heart. I rocked in bed to ground myself, to remind myself that I was an adult, but also to stay in the moment to see what I could learn about my abused child.

WRITING PROMPT:

When you re-live any kind of sensation or moment of the abuse, can you allow yourself to grab for your journal, and push through to simply jot down the sensations in your body? You don't have to write full sentences. Just the feelings. Cold. Dry ice. Punched in the heart. It is possible the anxiety attacks are because you became emotionally shut down, angry, cold, used addictive substances to make you feel better. Write what fits to your scenario.

To wait for an abuser is no joke. There can be periodic chills of memory. I consistently kept a man in my bed for my whole adult life because it was my comfort zone. I slept alone almost every night in the past four years to trip up the conditioning. I'm still learning to sleep over my boyfriend's house. While I can fall asleep in seconds at my home, when I sleep with him, I am almost instinctively on high alert. I don't want to sleep alone the rest of my life. I do hope to re-learn how to be in bed with a man I love clean now and clear from the secret. Yet, like any other transition with the abuse, it will take its time. One day when I fully share my bed with someone on a daily basis again, it will be in joy, not fearful defense. These body memories are the real deal. They are not to be taken lightly, and the person you spend your life with as you continue the path of recovery must know that sometimes you have triggers. For me it is anxiety attacks and that is a continual journey of unraveling. There could be different experiences around the corner. If I am open, and I trust God, I can make it through.

WRITING PROMPT:

What are the triggers for you in healing from the abuse? If not anxiety attacks, are there other impulses or ways to set you apart from others? Please don't beat yourself up for what you do to cope in healing, but I urge you to write about each episode so you can trace a pattern, and make one small move to interrupt it.

Instead of staying small from the anxiety attacks, I took time to learn about me and love myself in a way I hadn't ever allowed. I took trips to Big Sur and stayed in a monastery and picked fennel and lettuces in the Esalen gardens. I rode my bike in a bikini top in the sun on the bike path to the beach, and ditched the bike in the sand to take a quick swim in the waves. I went to movies alone. I spent all day on the couch reading a great book. The anxiety attacks started to abate. Life was starting to clean itself up. I had some real amazing eye opening epiphanies in my life. I had met some guy. I was nine months sober. I had moved on from Trader Joes to a substitute teacher at my kids' school making an honest wage. Passing the CBEST test to become a sub was one of the most grueling academic endeavors I had taken on in a very long time. I was taught in AA to take direction so I studied my ass off, re-learning 6th grade math. While I had failed all the practice tests, in the exam room, I had a moment with God.

"God, I have failed all the practice tests. I could fail this exam. If you want me to be a sub teacher, you will help me pass. If you don't, then I will fail and I am fine with that." Then I got busy with the test.

I passed with high marks and received my certification. As an added God shot bonus, leaving the testing facility, I ran into the ex-boyfriend who I had sex with unwillingly. I really enjoyed telling him I was going to be a teacher. I was a little stunned he was in the neighborhood because he was going to become a Rabbi. Horny rabbi, I thought.

"Let's get together some time," he said, shaking my hand. You could see on his face he knew… I was stronger now and not having any of his kind.

Sub teaching was working out great – I had a new sense of compassion for what my children experience all day, the grind of elementary public school. Ugh. It really brought me closer to their experience. I was on the path of recovery, and I was convinced the anxiety attacks were behind me for good. I felt like the God I now understood was my partner and the rest of the way was up. No more hold ups. Life would sky rocket.

Then the boyfriend suddenly dumped me by email because his life was too chaotic to have me in it. As this was my first sober relationship, there was no drugs or alcohol to quell my despair. I was plunged into bouts of the most ferocious anxiety attacks I had ever experienced. This level of love, still formative, brought on the mother lode of pain. The rejection and abandonment of my abuser returned.

The anxiety attacks hit standing before the little kids in the classroom. I felt strangled, a thumb pressing on my throat. I couldn't breathe, I couldn't swallow, I could only think about the chest crushing pressure and how I was going to die. Yet, I was so good in my life at putting on a game face even in the most cellular pain, I could make it through each day. I knew if there was alcohol around I would have ripped out the cork and downed as much as possible to make this feeling go away. Luckily there was no alcohol in the kindergarten room.

WRITING PROMPT:

Write an account of what your anxiety attack looks like from start to finish. Try and tap into the early sensations as it ramps up, through the eye of the storm and out to where it abates. Read this account to someone so they can be a witness and take the power away from the secrecy of it.

During my lunch break, I walked and prayed to God, please God, please God help me through this. I recalled being a small child in my bed and praying the same way to God. This was childhood anxiety that had been dormant and squashed. I was no longer a helpless child. I had children of my own. I needed to take back my life. No guy was going to take that from me. I saw I had a Santa Claus relationship with God. My connection with him could not just be when I wanted something, or to be saved. It had to be pervading and always.

I had that opportunity a few nights later. I was in the midst of a whopper anxiety attack, and I reached out to a woman in AA that I knew practiced a strong spiritual program while battling anxiety. She told me my throat was not going to close up permanently. I wasn't going to die. I needed to breathe and she took ten long breaths with me. No one in my life had ever sat and taken any breaths with me before. As I calmed down, we started to talk about acceptance of the anxiety. How would it be if I were to live my life knowing I had this all the time? Instead of fighting it? Fearing it? I could be bigger than my fear, she told me. I talked about standing up to the voice, the anxiety voice, the mean voice. I even ventured to say The Devil. I thought, I may not want to scream and yell senselessly at people I love anymore, but I can have permission to be brutal with the voice that causes my anxiety. Shut up you motherfucker. There is no room for you in my life anymore. You are not my God. You are the devil. I won't believe in you anymore.

That fellow read me a poem at that moment that I needed to hear:

Do not be anxious about ANYTHING but in EVERYTHING by prayer and petition, with THANKSGIVING (say it, ask for it and be in gratitude), present your requests to God. And the PEACE of God, which transcends all understanding, will guard your heart and your MIND in Christ Jesus. Phil 4:4-7.

She also sent me this beautiful meditation that really got my wheels spinning about spirit and owning your protection of your spirit:

"I will be more afraid of spirit – unrest, of soul – disturbance, or any ruffling of the mind, than of earthquake or fire. When I feel the calm of my spirit has been broken by emotional upset, then I must steal away alone with God, until my heart sings and all is strong and calm again. Uncalm times are the only times when evil can find an entrance. I will beware of unguarded spots of unrest. I will try to keep calm, no matter what turmoil surrounds me."

WRITING PROMPT:

Have your anxiety attacks come and gone? What is the story of your anxiety attacks? If they don't look or feel like mine, how do you manage the gnawing edge in your body? Imagine yourself recovered from anxiety over your abuse forever. What does that person feel like, and where would they be?

The anxiety attacks went away again for a bunch of months. I fell into thinking it was possible once again they were gone forever until one Saturday morning I had an anxiety attack that floored me. Despite consistently positive thought patterns, I was in a place this particular morning of disbelief. I had let the old thoughts of a scared damaged woman come into my beautiful Saturday morning. I had lost trust in the spiritual path that brought me to where I was and instead was spinning out in a place of loneliness and lack of love. Many sexual abuse survivors believe they are terminally alone due to the nastiness of their secrets, and they block themselves from connection due to habit.

Typically I would hide in shame from all anxiety attacks especially from my kids. I would distract them with the TV and go in my room and hold myself and shake. This time, I was not interested in hiding. I slid down the side of my bed and calmly allowed the tears to cascade down my face. When my kids found me, and they did because they always need to know where the art scissors are, or to get my weigh in on an argument or to ask for a glass of water, I told them in a safe and loving way that I was okay and just having feelings. At this moment, it was imperative that I had this experience intimately with my kids. They were my family and it was time to be okay with being a fully human mommie in front of them. To be okay with us, the three of us, as a family unit. I had not burned down all the walls of family. I was not some damaged harlot of hell. I was a woman trying to get not just back on her feet, but to live her biggest dreams after coping with sexual abuse. Sometimes it all moved too fast and I had to slow down.

I told them my chest hurt, and it would pass. They brought me water and a tissue and smoothed my hair. They were obviously concerned at ten and six years old, but I showed them in a safe sane way that adults have vulnerable moments. After I recovered, I was swept over by complete joy. We went to the farmers market in the sunshine and bought avocados and goat cheese and went to my favorite candle store in Los Angeles, Stone Candle. The owner has an ice cream cooler and the girls ate free ice cream sandwiches at 10AM.

We smelled candles and infused oils for our burner at home. It was like the sunrise after the perfect storm.

While it was the abuse emerging that led me to anxiety, it was the most organic pathway to show my kids it's okay to be their fullest messy selves. When they had feelings or anxiety, how could I tell them that they didn't have the right to stand in their own discomforts and power after they witnessed mine?

WRITING PROMPT:

Do people you love witness your anxiety or depression? If you don't suffer directly from either, do you repress your feelings in anger or silence? Do you feel obligated to alleviate discomfort for your loved ones when you are processing?

The best part of all is I was not angry that this random anxiety attack happened after none for so long. Instead I was so grateful that my body and mind could help me see I was out of spiritual and creative alignment with the rest of my beautiful life. *You have gotten ahead of yourself in your head*, I was warned. I would need to be on vigilant patrol at all times that my mind wasn't hijacked by my own mind. That is the gateway to anxiety attacks. When I am running too fast and hard. When I am not fully present in the middle of the miracle of my life.

Sexual abuse healing and the anxiety attacks exposed my blind spots in my belief in God. I had a lot of problems with God during early recovery because I still felt he was doing this to my life in some way. I prayed like a crazy person to God when I was in the throes of attacks. I may have prayed really hard to God when I was being abused too. He was listening, but to a child, that is impossible to understand when something doesn't stop. My fractured soul revealed all the places where I dialed God in without true connection because of a deeper doubt.

I went through a phase I call "dueling spirituality." Good versus evil. I had to rewrite my childish perceptions of God. Before I could see that there could be a strong and positive good that wanted to lift me up to the brightest life light, I had to create the fact that evil wants to come in when we allow our soul of spirit to be weak with fear and anxiety. I had the tendency to allow the evil to be stronger than the spirit of God, and so I needed to fight it and dispel it before I could look towards the sun. For me, the evil wanted to take me out front and center, away from my life purpose. This thinking was based on there being a God, and then there was my dad. So I started to slowly take away the evil force as an adult, and understand there was just God. There was no room for evil. It was just my old thinking.

I had tried to have a relationship with God my whole life that was bargaining. Give me this and I will be good. To God I already was perfect. There was no good or bad. He just wanted me to feel loved.

WRITING PROMPT:

Write out your plea bargain with God. If you don't have a God, who do you plead to in your recovery? Do you want to bypass pain?

I don't focus now on evil forces but I know that energies lurk that want to take me out. Those energies are in the form of doubt and shame, and they are the opposite of my God. Evil looks like any form of fear that makes me believe I can't have everything I want in life when there is no real evidence to that truth. It's just my distorted thinking. When I started this book as a spiritual tool and guide for abuse survivors, I was at a phase in my discovery and acceptance of my abuse where I was not yet connecting to spirituality. How would I be able to convey teachings or observances to other survivors if I have no faith? The anxiety attacks were my spirit standing up to point out that I related to bad more than good, and in order to be a teacher, I had to believe good was my source. I had to open up my heart.

If you currently have anxiety attacks, I know it is hard to read that I am appreciating them or that they have something to do with me finding God. Trust me, through two years of constant anxiety attacks I did not appreciate them at all. I hated them. Now when

I get one, I am informed. I have to get back in constant contact with God, let out a good cry, call a witness, and re-up my sense of presence and self. The anxiety attack is telling me what I am not experienced enough to see. That my life is happening in an amazing way and I am trying to race through it and erase the moments as they pass.

Today, I need "thought vigilance." Abuse survivors need this more than people who were not abused, especially in times when life presents new big juicy opportunities. Once I feel the tingle of an attack, I have already done the negative thinking that got it started. You can't turn back time. You can't pray anxiety attacks away. You have to let the vapors of old thought burn off and through you. New experiences in life, bigger challenges of new thinking need vigilant belief and prayer. The anxiety attacks may never go away, but I don't need to live in fear of them as long as I step continuously into a bigger life.

WRITING PROMPT:

What debilitating behavior in your recovery path went away for a while and then came back? How did you handle its return? How was it different and how can you use that as a learning tool?

You are learning to survive in a different way than the survival of the abuse itself. Now you learn to survive the aftermath, the anxiety, the dark criticizing voices in your head, functioning in the real world with other people who were not abused, learning that one day you can trust. You will normalize. It will happen. It happened to me. It can happen to you. What you endure in the process of getting to the other side produces in your heart a love and awareness that will bring a new kind of tears to pour down your face. Tears of love, happiness and whole connection.

God is just getting my attention the best way he can through my soul. Through the body I need to claim back as my own without the residual memories of abuse. With rigorous focus on my thoughts, I can, with my higher source, heal my soul.

CHAPTER FIVE
THERAPY: THE GOOD,
THE BAD, THE UGLY

Before I uncovered the truth about the sexual abuse in my child-hood, I thought I had a "sex problem." My best thinking was "Let's fix that." Weary of the pattern of using my body as my best asset, I sought relief. A friend referred me to a male therapist who specialized in sex issues.

"He's very insightful with long time sobriety. He may help you without charging too much," she said.

When I walked out of the room after our introductory session and he looked at my ass, I knew he was not the man to help me come to terms with a "sex problem."

I had met another very nice female therapist but there was some-thing about her room with the toys and the dolls that freaked me out. I was in such deep denial about the sexual abuse, my ego self knew she would uncover secrets I didn't want to face. She wouldn't just talk about why I needed to get validation from my pussy so much. She would dig. I told her I wasn't ready. I think I blamed money. I wasn't ready to be saved. I had to live in the turmoil a bit longer.

Ass-checking male therapist became a part of my journey to get better, albeit in a very dysfunctional way. A few days after our meeting, he asked me out. Since my only real criteria at this point for dating men was their desire for me, I said yes. My disconnection from my feelings made me dangerously naïve. I was married most of my adult life so dating hadn't been an agenda. The therapist had money from his business ventures and wanted to spend it on me … while we got dirty. Sounds like solid boyfriend material, right? Flashback to my dad visiting me in college, buying dinners and throwing one hundred dollar bills my way. Abuse pay off. So I was just acting that out with this guy. Rather than get real therapy, I decided I could "work out" my sexual issues by having "good sex". It never dawned on me that a) I had just sat in a room with this man and told him all my sexual proclivities and weaknesses and b) it was kind of morally unethical for him to ask me out as a therapist knowing these secrets. But again, I had no self-worth or awareness, so we started a relationship that involved a considerable amount of fucking, and he bought me a coffee maker, Ugg boots and a Kindle.

I consciously used his full desire to have a lot of sex with me to vet that deprived part of me still lingering from the last bunch of years in my marriage where sex had become very contentious. I used him to explore my sexuality, an unrealized place I had never been. He was not a bad man, or an unsafe man, he ended up being quite good to me at a time I was really in a low place as a single mother working at a supermarket. He also took me to a few AA meetings and we worked for a charity on Thanksgiving. One day about four months in I knew he wasn't my guy. His belittling behaviors had gotten to me, and when I called him out about them, he told me I just wanted to shame him. I broke up with him and moved on. I had never done that in four months time. I usually married people!

It was three months later when I had the first dream of abuse that brought me to call my ex-marriage counselor and her to refer me to Rena, the therapist who would change my life. While I knew exactly what the dream was telling me, my denial had been in place for so long I wasn't going into therapy ready to flip the switch and operate my life as an incest survivor. I was not going to pick up that label and run with it so easy. She had her work cut out for her.

WRITING PROMPT:

Have you started therapy of some kind for your abuse? What were the feelings in the first session? If you haven't started therapy, why?

My sexual abuse secret lay dormant my whole life until this point partially because I hadn't encountered intuitive therapists. In my twenties I saw a lovely elderly lady referred by my mom who enjoyed our talks more than giving me therapy. She even asked me to read her book. I would write sometimes in her office. She never detected abuse. I find that hard to believe as she was highly respected in her field. I went to a couple's therapist with my second husband after we had my first daughter and she didn't detect the abuse. She just thought we had drained our "love banks." She had us do exercises like turning to each other and telling each other what we loved about each other. It didn't stick. Of course it didn't. The dark secret of abuse was raging under my skin. When your own mother stuffs it under her own roof, how can you ever know truly?

I then tried an analyst, a male, in another city we lived in, and he was useless. I knew that I needed some therapy though. It had been fifteen years. I knew I was slowly going crazy in my mind, but I didn't know why. When my now ex husband and I moved back to LA with our two daughters, we tried another couple's therapist and she was excellent, but we had already done to much damage to the marriage. I used the sessions to get my own therapy. Unfortunately, therapy without revealing the abuse was like baling water out of a rapidly sinking boat.

By the time I sat before my sexual abuse therapist, I was at the bottom. Divorced single parent, I saw my career in film as an abject failure. I feared reality and the unknown. I loathed the entertainment industry because it represented my imposter self. When I left the movies, I left with my old story and was scared there was no alternative to being a storyteller (so I was mourning that loss). My sexual appetite was voracious, like the abuse had made me a sexual monster when the case was I just was acting out a lot in lieu of having control over my mind and body connection. Yet, as I embraced the little girl who had been shown sexuality in the early formative years, I yearned for a new kind of sex that was intimate, loving and caring. I questioned if my therapist could handle all these issues.

WRITING PROMPT:

What therapists have come and gone in your life? Can you see where they have been either right or wrong for you? If you are looking for a therapist, write out what you are looking for to share with them. Interview them. This is a vital partnership for recovery.

I wanted to be ready to have all of my feelings intact to talk about before I went into my first therapy session so I did what I know…I wrote my ass off. This was the real deal: Sexual Abuse Therapy. It felt a little daunting. I struggled with voices in my head that told me I was being overdramatic! Maybe it's not as bad as you think. Do you really need to be so committed to this "concept?" Suddenly my whole lifetime of fighting the dark secret of incest became like an annoying itch. I found my writing trying to minimize the issue. Well, now that you know, is there more to discover? The words on the page would taunt me. I believe I did this to protect myself from disappointment with the therapist in case she was like all the rest. She wouldn't see the real me. She wouldn't believe me even if I told her.

I would have it all figured out BEFORE I got into therapy so there were no surprises. Yet, I craved reveals and surprises. I would take anything different than the reality I had lived in up to this point. I was going to be a hard nut to crack; still a scrappy angry kid under the glamour and smarts. I wanted to take a bat to shit. No one had ever let me stew, but to their defense, I was such an explosive raging person. I scared myself sometimes with my capacity for anger. My therapist would be the first person to engage me in sexual abuse dialogue. She would see me as mad as one could be. I prayed she could handle it.

WRITING PROMPT:

Are you a perfectionist? Do you feel judged if you don't have all the answers? Write a situation where you allowed yourself to not know the outcome and what that felt like.

The first day I went into therapy, I was split in two. On one hand, I was so unbelievably relieved I had finally come to this conclusion that I was potentially (note, I was still not convinced) abused, but I also felt incredibly silly. Like I had made up this ailment because I had run out of reasons why my life was never getting to that full glorious place I knew it could be at one day. My relationship with my therapist would be like none other I had ever had. It didn't take long for the floodgates to open once I saw I my therapist wouldn't doubt me. Memories of drives in the dark, hushed words, quiet visits, the pleasure, the confusion, the desire, the torment and anger. All in a small seven year old body. They came fast and hard.

She was never judgmental about anything I said or how hard I cried or when I choked, gagged, got red in the face and went into catatonia. When she did give her opinion, she often accepted my resistance. She spent a lot of the first six months watching me just sob and vent in disbelief and terror in her office. I would leave so despondent. I would be on the street in Santa Monica on a sunny Tuesday afternoon and feel like a warped lost alien. The world was a weapon. There was no safe space. I can tell you while that happened for many months during therapy, I started to get my footing and I would leave feeling like I had gained something versus being ground down like glass.

I worked out my anger at my mother on my therapist by expressing how much it sucked that she didn't protect me, or love me enough as a kid. That maybe if she had spent more time in consciousness in her life, she would have intercepted what was going on in her daughter's bed. I was able through my therapist to experience what it is like to have a woman listen to you and believe you. To not discount your feelings.

A few months into the therapy, I had another dream. My dad was in some long old 1960's sedan picking me up at this retreat I had been on as a child. He was in a trench coat, and I knew I didn't want to get in the car with him. I also would be leaving the boy I had met on the retreat; my first innocent crush. I was able to reveal to my therapist I that I had never told anyone in the context of abuse about this wonderful family camp I attended when I was maybe seven or eight. The dates are blurry for me, as was the place, but I knew it was a Baha'i Retreat. I had met the blond boy who was my first crush. I can recall the feeling of total euphoria when I ran around the grassy fields and knolls with him that summer visit. The innocence and the balance of our youth. I now understood that sinking hideous feeling of having to get back in the car at the end of the retreat with my dad and go back home where I wasn't protected and be plunged back into adult relations. To go back to where the male world was old and mature and sexual and scary. I wanted to stay with the young boy.

I knew I had to see a picture of this place so I kept praying to recall its name. One day it came to me as Green Acres in Maine. When I saw the picture of the place, tears fells down my eyes. I emailed the enrollment director. Do they have any kind of roster of kids that were there in 1976? They didn't. They told me there were some groups that were alumni. They wished me luck. I wasn't able to find that boy, but it was a key memory to start the process of realizing as a small child what was taken from me with the abuse. It also started me really thinking about how young I was that I wanted to escape into young boys and get away from the image of my father and sexuality.

WRITING PROMPT:

Do you have fanciful and free memories of your childhood where you were safe for a time from the abuse?

I think my ten-year old self couldn't bear the absence of the abuse when it ended. It was so tragic and triggering to me. If you think about it, if you are loved a certain way by someone, then it ends, you are cut off. The secret dies in the silence and the loneliness. I don't recall the day the abuse ended, but I bet it wasn't a mistake that I positioned myself in my life in most of my romantic relationships so that I was the one that ended it. I would make sure no one would leave me again.

I had boyfriends from age twelve forward, and started drugs and alcohol by thirteen. It was a long repression my therapist and I would be unraveling.

WRITING PROMPT:

Do you remember when the abuse ended and how you felt? I am aware this may be impossible for some people. I personally don't recall the day itself, but when I lean into the page, I can recall the free falling state. See where the moment takes you.

There were waves of recalling the essence of abuse in my therapy, mostly the touching, but the memories were never graphic or specific. They may be down there buried. I may one day want to remember more but I think it would require EMDR or some kind of hypnosis because it is lodged in a place that is beyond my mouth speaking. It is possible I had disassociated so well from my body, left my body, in those moments, that the actual recall was too hard to make now forty years later. I just knew the day I staggered into that therapy session broken and beaten down by an angry life of substance abuse and sexual manipulation with men (as well as lack of sexual self care for myself), I couldn't go on living my life this way. I was tired, and angry. I didn't like how I was with my kids – unpredictable and sometimes aggressive. I had a string of failed relationships after my second marriage. When my kids would go to their dads, I spent a lot of afternoons clutching my journal on my bed, writing and weeping. In fact, I spent a fair amount of time in bed during early recovery from sexual abuse. Just hiding on some days when the world felt a little too vast and large.

WRITING PROMPT:

Write about what it feels like to be "sick" in bed, even if it is emotionally depressed. Do you allow yourself this healing without judgment? Write from a third person you, looking at your vulnerable sick self. Do you feel unattended, trapped, lonely? Can you care for the sad sick you today?

When I started sexual abuse counseling, I was in a relationship with a man twenty years older than me. He was twenty-five years sober, very gentle, eager to please, and we dated and traveled for a year. My therapist worked with me through the relationship. She never judged me or labeled it. I would joke I was doing the "daddy thing." In fact she and my sex and love addicts anonymous sponsor were supportive of it. I wasn't being harmed and he was kind to my children (who loathed him and made it really clear...poor guy!). He was pivotal as someone to be in my life to work out these very early abuse recovery triggers. I was also still drinking and so I had sex triggered in a messy way at times with him.

At one point we were going away on a weekend to a hotel, and an hour before he picked me up, I panicked. I recall standing in my bedroom that was covered with plastic and tarps because I was painting the walls. It was like a sterile room for the insane.

I called my therapist sobbing.

"I can't go," I said. "I think he's a pedophile and I can't date a pedophile because he may hurt my kids."

This man had never indicated he was a pedophile in any way, except for one time he alluded to how young teens are so much more now into sex than before, like he has seen in "videos." I had searched up a young teen girl video and painfully watched some barely conscious teen girl touch herself in an amateur video. It enraged me, his ignorance to those girls putting on a show and really having no connection to their young exploited bodies. You sick fuck, I thought. You have no clue, and I have daughters. I told my therapist this was the basis of not going on the weekend.

"I don't see it how you do," she said. "I would go on the weekend. And ask him about it."

I took a risk, went away with him and told him about what I had thought. He was offended at first, but did not discount my feelings and fears. I saw that he was simply from a generation who had no clue in this new video era and he led a fairly sheltered sexual life. He had seen one video and had made an assumption. My relationship with him was the very tip of my practice of starting to talk openly with male partners about what was happening for me inside. It was all unresolved inner child stuff that wasn't going to necessarily exist forever in a relationship. It was not so fun to be with me when I wanted to talk about this stuff. It was a definite buzz kill to the healthy "get to know you" phase, or to own my power and confidence in the subsequent "what's next" phase of the relationship. Also, I was still growing, and I outgrew our future. I walked away from that relationship shocked at my ability to say "No thank you. This is not enough for me." I chose my preference over any male hook. I thought I left him because I was looking for better, a deeper soul mate … but I yet still to fall in love with the soul mate in me.

What facing my fears and feelings with men did was it led me to see my very important position as a mother to have eyes wide open to protect my own daughters from any harm by not being in the denial my mom was, or any other women in my family. Someone had to know. I had an aunt who has passed now, my mom's sister, and I have a hunch she was abused by my grandfather. I feel like sometimes she saw through me and knew. But how could she discuss my secret if hers was buried deep too? I have broken the chain by getting help and that is one of the truest gifts of suffering.

I worked with my therapist every week for a couple years. Some of the stretches of time we talked about trust issues and every day coping mechanisms. Then there were the sessions where I was actually bored, and thought maybe I don't need therapy anymore. I am wasting my time and money. I have peaked in my revelations. Translation: a colossal breakthrough was right around the corner.

WRITING PROMPT:

Have you had moments in therapy where you felt like nothing was happening and then there was a big breakthrough? Document those sessions so you can have more faith in therapy's nature course.

In recovery they say, don't leave before the miracle happens. I stayed in therapy longer than I wanted to because I had a hunch there was more to remember, to walk through. Some days I wanted to quit. "Enough suffering!" I would think. Our old self wants to continue to protect us because it doesn't think we can handle any more truth. It creates exit strategies to get us out because when we were abused we had none. We couldn't leave. We had to stay till it was over so we used our brain to exit the situation. We need as adults to tell the little inner child brain we have a handle on this now so we can go deeper. Make the magic. Find the solutions. Step into a life bigger, vaster and more abundant than we could ever imagine.

When I wrote about my bigger life, and explored my desires, the scope was small. I was floundering when God led me to the job as a substitute teacher. Being around the innocence of children all day helped me see what being a child was like. In the present, I mourned my childhood, dropped daily into a hectic loud environment of elementary school like I was normal. Like I wasn't carrying the secret of abuse. Walking into schools every day and standing before children as an educating adult chipped away at my own inner child's terror of survival. My heart built an inner strength that eroded a darker weakness established for so many decades. Continuing therapy through new experiences of visibility and change was a smart decision because I couldn't make sense of my new life on my own.

When we don't face our trauma, we bury it with addictions. For me it was booze, pot, perfectionism, anger, shame and sex. The truth is we have expectations of how life is going to be, because we have been in that mindset for so long we don't know how to see any other way, or believe there is another way to live out there for us. For me, my skin would crawl in sobriety and this was especially when I took time away from sex with men to heal. I had the potential to really fall into a trap of not giving a shit about my body. I also had the opportunity to hate everyone around me for how much my skin felt like it was crawling all the time. My therapist held incredible space as I went through this intense time of surrender.

"I don't want to be in this body anymore," I sobbed to her in one session. "It's ravaged and abused and torn and it doesn't fit where my mind is growing and going."

I was outgrowing my body and since I had no relationship with the mind/body connection, I couldn't connect with my new shell. My soul needed this body to grow and prosper so I had to change how I treated it and shared it. In this body, I had to learn how to have the right to exist and trust I didn't have to give the body away to any substance or man. A psychic told me recently that I could handle a lot of people's stuff and big egos and I don't need to worry about what they think of me, or try and please them. I took that to heart and embodied it. I would make this body work by aligning it to my healthier mind.

WRITING PROMPT:

Explore how your body feels and looks to you today. When do you admire it the most, and what parts of it excite you? I personally love my shoulders, arms and ribs. They feel sexy and I understand they are part of my beautiful body.

If you are still lying in the bathtub during the day—which I did many times in the first year of abuse recovery, sometimes twice a day if I felt really unsafe—you will eventually bathe your body in honor of it walking you through a life full of bounty and beauty. I had epiphanies in that tub that informed me I was finally getting well after being sick MY WHOLE LIFE. I was abused in infancy so I had been abused the whole first decade of life. One package of lavender Epsom salts and burning sage wasn't going to make that truth go away fully but they sure could take the power out of it for one hour one day at a time.

I questioned my therapist many times in this process. Maybe she isn't deep enough ... Do we chat about my kids too much in our sessions? I think she should do more inner child work. I should be sobbing and freaking out every time I go in, not just once a month. I was honest with her about my concerns. I had to be. I was practicing using my voice to get what I wanted and needed in my recovery. I eventually stopped going to therapy when I was fully neutral with the decision I was complete. I did not get terrorized over the memories of abuse any longer, and could identify the feelings associated to abuse trauma in my life when they arose. I was tired of rehashing the same thought pattern again and again. I was ready to apply my findings to life. My therapist questioned whether I was ready, but standing my ground put me on another level of confidence and taking back my power. It was a choice and I made it clean. I had options in life. If I chose to not do therapy for a while and needed to go back, I knew where to find her. She would be there waiting with open arms. I know if I do go back, it would be for a new layer and I would approach the discovery with curiosity and not fear.

I have a lot of support in my community. It is essential for people who have been abused to not have too much time alone. Over the three years of recovery, I have leaned on sponsors and fellows in two twelve step programs, a business coach, life coach, branding coach, networking groups, listening partnerships, dating and friendships. I also love the time I have seeing my clients walk through their pain and grow. I am not a therapist but I do help them heal through writing. My recovery brought me to the truth of my gift. My clients in return each teach me in divine timing what I need to know about love, money, comedy and truth. When I think I am unique in my problems, there is always someone with a different perspective/ same problem, or someone who has it far worse.

Sure, some days I wonder if I need therapy again, but I have enough self-reliance that if I do, it won't be a conflict in my mind. It will be a clear choice for my health. Today I employ few coaches, have deeper friendships, connect daily with God, but most importantly, trust my inner voice like never before. When old thoughts and fears come rushing in, wanting to make you small, reach out to other women, cry and get honest. Say, I feel fucked up. This is what I am thinking about my boyfriend, money, my kids. They can tell you, "Girl, take a nap and eat something, pause and reset." 100% of the time they are right. You can get your astounding and exciting life back in less than an hour when you use your voice, and know you have choices.

Time speeds up, and yet time is exactly what it's supposed to be.

We have no control, but we have all the control. We have choices when we get help.

Choice sets us free.

Chapter Six
Telling Others

To never divulge my abuse, I lived a teen into adult life of escapism with alcohol, pot, rage, co-dependence, sexual fantasy and career obsession, all while keeping up a front that I was simply a high-achiever.

At one point, mid my abuse recovery it became clear that even though I was down to a couple glasses of wine and a cigarette a night, an alcohol obsession was blocking me from ultimate clarity and voice about my abuse. When I walked into AA one year after I started sexual abuse counseling, I surrendered that I needed to clean up my act if my life was going to monumentally change. I admitted I was an alcoholic. I needed to talk about the abuse in connection with why I escaped in drugs and alcohol. I benefitted from the open space to share for clarity, support and peace. It also brought me closer to God.

I also knew I wanted to shift how or I shared this part of me with men. I had been in a couple relationships where it was pretty front and center. What would a relationship look like if it was known, but as part of information gathering versus this big bag of terror and crap I revealed like a load onto the relationship. Also, what did my new sexuality look like, and how could I hold that as clean and clear with a man who knew I had been abused?

WRITING PROMPT:

Have you had a chance to take a look at your sexuality free from the binds of the abuse history? Write about what would a sexual encounter clear and free from the binds of abuse look like. Get as racy as you want! Unlock your unique desires!

I had a four-month period of aloneness where I could come to terms with the new me. I bought a bike and in the summer would ride the path to the beach in my bikini top and park the bike by the beach and swim and just feel the freedom of taking simple actions. I would go to movies. I ceased putting my energy into performing for men. I didn't lap dance a man in slutty lingerie so he'd love me. I didn't show my sexual prowess after dinner by straddling my date in the car on the side of the PCH. There was no more, look at me! I am so sexually fascinating and free! I can give head while you're driving! I am so bold! Instead I would take sometimes two baths in one day. I would call women and sob and ask them how I could love myself. I couldn't fathom dating someone and having to ever tell them again I was an incest survivor. I thought, I will never know how to do this. I didn't want to do this.

Then I had a breakthrough. I started to honor myself. Sexual abuse went from being something a man who was with me had to know, to a discussion reserved for a special loving long-term relationship. I got better at dating men even four times without saying a word. It was long enough to see we were not a match, and I had held my own as the woman I am today, not some injured fractured little girl self. That happened because my emotional support circle had widened giving me the space to talk freely about the abuse and how it affected my day to day well being versus sharing it with men. I could also lean on prayer with God before dates and ask even if it is the fifth date and I get nervous for courage not tell out of shame or some self fulfilling prophecy that they will see me as damaged anyway. I had one three-month relationship and I dropped the abuse bomb over eggs at breakfast. It landed so awkwardly and poorly that I learned about time and place to share something so deep. I also saw his lack of capacity to hold emotional space for me. Either that or it just didn't matter. I started to see it was my old story, and how or if I carried it into my dating life needed to be re-examined. I didn't need to be silent, but I also no longer needed to wave the flag.

WRITING PROMPT:

What was it like for you to tell partners? Did you find it easy or shaming? Write out the conversation you would eventually love to have.

I told my estranged sister before I told my mom. I thought I was going to help her but I think, since we hadn't talked in a few years due to a falling out, that I was using it to trauma bond. I wanted her to know that perhaps this was why she hated me so much, why we were all so broken. I know that we did not see eye to eye in some areas, or she didn't feel like I loved her enough, but she had not talked to me in four years. I had a hunch she may need to know for her own discovery, so I asked if we could speak. I wasted no time, and got right to the point.

"I am facing the fact that I was sexually abused for a long time by our dad."

I waited with held breath for her response. It was not what I expected.

"That explains everything," she said.

That was exactly what my ex husband had said. I was seeing a pattern with the people in my past.

Besides a few birthday texts, we haven't talked about the call that day. I pray that one day, because of time and healing, we will come together again and talk now that I am no longer in denial.

I couldn't heal the people who had been in my path when I was an angry abuse victim in denial. I continued to keep the focus on me and behave in love and integrity. I was not responsible to heal my ex-husband from the tumultuous time we were together in my abuse denial and addictions. We were two storms together and we beat the hell out of each other emotionally. There was something in him attracted to me in that state. Now he can have a new per-spective of his life, and I can be a fair and kind co-parent. When I was in that raw first year of facing alcoholism and abuse, I needed women who could teach me to hug myself and hold space for me as I sobbed and sobbed. In the second year, I was looking more for people who could appreciate that I had suffered trauma but was looking for a closer connection to God to have a stronger and bigger life. I also needed to tell my story to give other men and women the courage to speak. The way I told was changing dramatically in a short period of time when I committed to unearthing all the feelings and facts.

Before I could talk to my mom, I had to think about whether I thought she knew and if she didn't say she knew, what I would do with that answer. Would I be in acceptance? Every time I thought of telling her, I loathed her so much for not protecting me. I spent a year writing about my abuse without approaching her until I was in a place of neutrality. It was empowering to document the unraveling of my old self, and the reconstruction of my new life without attacking anyone about it. I wanted my story clear for other people still suffering, and therefore I had to follow the timeline of when the words would tell me my next action. They did. As the book took shape, I would find myself in new directions, actions, and eventually, stepping into a bigger life.

WRITING PROMPT:

Be consistent in writing about your recovery so you can tell it to other men and women who need your experience, strength and hope. If you haven't, it is never too late to start. Let the words of each day take you into the new direction without forcing it.

Before I told my mom, I needed to tell another woman. God puts people in our path who have already coped with the abuse and can be conduits for our healing. At the end of 2014 I was working on a television project with a confident beautiful woman, a mother of two who had been married for twenty years to a doting man. The writing sessions were in her home when the kids were at school, and she always had some kind of yummy home baked dish prepared like enchiladas or quinoa casserole. Due to the comforts of home surrounding me, I felt open and intimate in this relationship. We would talk about our personal lives; indicative of writing relationships. One day I announced to her that I had been sexually abused by my dad.

"I was abused," she said not missing a beat.

I stared at her shocked. "Really?"

She nodded. "Yup. By multiple perpetrators when I was younger."

She had everything. She was a model, a mother, a businesswoman. You would never know. It made me realize how many women out there had potentially been abused that didn't talk about it at all. This woman was strong. She didn't take crap from anyone.

"Did you tell your mom?" I asked.

"Sure," she said. "But she didn't really have a reaction."

"When did you know," I asked, on the edge of my seat.

"In my early twenties. I moved on from my mother's ambivalence," she said.

"I don't know when to tell my mom," I said, feeling bad that I had wasted my whole life harboring my secret.

"You'll know when you are ready because it will be easy."

I remember the afternoon I was ready. I was sitting in a coffee shop on the West side of Los Angeles working and the voice hit me like a thunderbolt.

You have to write your mom the email right now.

I had someone I could be accountable to, who could support me. I knew once I emailed my mom my secret, I could go back to my friend and she would hold me powerful. She was a woman my age, a mom, and she had done it. I could do it too.

The email just flowed out of me. My heart was pounding out of my chest like a small scared child when I hit send. Then I emailed my friend;

"I sent it."

She immediately sent me an email back:

"Now go live and make what you want from life a reality!"

I left the restaurant and sobbed in my car. She was right. It was time to be set free and this was just the beginning.

My mom's reaction to the email was one of sympathy. She wanted to talk on the phone. She said she had never known and she was so sorry. My feelings were split between empathy and blame. How could a mother not know her daughter was being sexually visited by her husband for a decade? In her youth, she was a very controlling person who operated from a place of rigor and perfectionism. It seemed so unfathomable that she never suspected anything. In fact, I recall her thinking my dad was cheating on her once. I witnessed a very traumatic fight between them. I think back now to me protecting my dad. Inside I was probably screaming, "It's not that woman he is having an affair with! It is me!" When she locked him out of the house, I was the one to let him in.

When I got on the phone with my mom, the first thing she said was "I am so sorry. I had no idea."

I could feel her struggling with the fact that her entire past, her own marriage, was disintegrating all around her. She was pushing through to honor my pain and the experience we were having being about me and my recovery. After we talked about it for a half hour or so, she said, "Now you can have your power back."

I hated her for it as much as I loved her for it. Honestly, I was just grateful she didn't deny it. I was fearful she would demand facts. Telling her and her reaction didn't really matter because this was for me, not for her. When she started to cry, there was no defensive position I could take. I just sat in the space and let her have her feelings.

The cloak of denial had hung as hard on her shoulders as it had on mine. We had that shared burden silently together for decades.

" I am not blaming you," I said to her. I knew if I wanted to continue to have a relationship with my mom, then I couldn't attack her.

"I know," she said.

"So..." I said. "What else is going on?" I felt the need to progress the conversation into some kind of mundane normalcy. That is the people pleaser in me. I still didn't know how to use my voice to say, "I need to get off the phone now and not act like this was just a normal catch up call." So I let her tell me for a little bit about her condo renovation and then we got off the phone.

I thought telling my mother was the whole journey. Boy was I wrong. For the year and a half that I struggled with do I tell her/do I not tell her and kept turning it over to God because I didn't know the definitive answer, I was growing and changing and putting into play what I was learning about life in sobriety from drugs, alcohol and sex and love addiction. Those were my crutches to shut out the terror that I had endured as a child. It took me decades to develop them, but only a couple years to quit them once I got serious about getting well inside. I have worked hard to forgive my mom, and to be the most loving daughter I can be as an example to my daughters so they can in turn be loving daughters when I grow old. When I visit my mom, I learn little nuggets that coincide with the dropping away of my anger and resentment, and the opening up of my awareness. We were at an Easter dinner and debating the benefit to teenage children want-ing you to pick them up places despite the late hour of midnight. I said I couldn't recall at all ever being picked up by a parent at that hour. My mom interjected and said that she had in fact picked me up … once for a dance to meet boys and the other time to sleep over a boy's house. I was shocked as I sat there that these were to two examples she could think of. Me with boys. I also thought of a few other times and they were always to go somewhere with a girlfriend to flirt with a boy.

Sitting at this dinner post-conversation, my mind wanted me to believe I was thrown to the wolves by my mom as a young girl. I was used at home by my dad as a sexual and emotional pillow, and she was driving me to other boys. Validation from a man had been imprinted on me at such a young age that it suffocated any natural impulses for my own substance and value. I had to fight for every-thing I wanted in life because the battle was waging inside me. It was unnatural to desire my self-worth outside a man because it was imbalanced in its development. When I square on faced this four decade affliction, I made a plan to clean house of that thinking. It wasn't my mom. It wasn't my dad. My happiness was now in my own hands. I could understand the seeds planted of the abuse. It wasn't a secret anymore. I didn't need to throw chairs and yell at an Easter dinner. I could just have compassion and forgive everyone for a time that was now long in the past. I could unlock the door of my life to more happiness.

WRITING PROMPT:

When was the first time you told a family member about the abuse? What went through your mind when you told?

The couple days following telling my mom, I was on the borderline of a complete nervous breakdown. I recall sitting in my car thinking, I can't do this. I can't handle all that is opening inside of me. I was sure I did not have the capacity to take on this truth, the lies, the loss of childhood, the lack of protection I was given. I wanted to fill my body with a whole bottle of wine quickly, and take lots of Valium. The problem was I was newly sober and what I truly needed was a soft blanket and pillow, and someone to make me food and hold me, and let me sleep and cry through the pain in a safe place. Besides, I hate Valium.

Instead I wrote a long desperate email to my newish boyfriend about how I was a "blank slate now." He had known I was telling my mom about it, and had been my first call after. I was scared he wouldn't like the new me. Again, I fell into the trap of the man's validation of me matters more than what is transforming inside me. He was not equipped to handle my experiences as he had his own emotional turmoil, but he was an easy target to completely over share. I learned in the future that the space to share your regurgitation of vulnerability, doubt, confusion and desperation is within strong support systems of other women and survivors. They are best equipped to hold you as your secret seeps out into your life's many corners. It is painful to meet the new you especially when none of these stages of processing the abuse appear to be leading to happiness. They are, and they do. I am a testament to that truth.

I have told a lot of people about the sexual abuse now. I have told a few old friends.

One cautionary tale is to be mindful of "trauma bonding" with the abuse. While a majority of my life started to be steeped in joy, satisfaction and simple peace, people from the past reappeared in the strangest ways; specifically men I had acted out sexually with in the dance of denial and self-hatred. For instance, I ran into a flame leaving a bookstore in Santa Monica right after a therapy session. It had been fifteen years. Our relationship back then was torrid, brief and overlapping the end of my first marriage.

"What a trip running into you're here," I said. He was not shy in looking me up and down through mirrored shades.

"You look great!" he said. "Are you dating anyone?"

"Nope, completely single," I said. I left out the part that I was on a one year hiatus from men. The lure of the past was too intoxicating.

We got together a week later for brunch, and in no less than ten minutes, were deep into trauma bonding. If you are not familiar with that term, it is when you get a rush, or an addictive sexual charge when recounting all your past "dirt" with a man who was part of the dirt. This time, though, I got to share about my sexual abuse, and he got share about his failed relationships. Soon we were making out in my car, fueled by a raw sexuality. God had put him back in my life not to be reunited, but to reflect on not wanting to be the old me and to stand up finally for who I am and how I want to be treated. That moment in the car felt so seedy and aggressive. I didn't feel safe. Instead I was crazed by a synthetic eroticism that I knew now to be not of this plane of joy I was on. It was the kind of sexuality that comes in denial and darkness.

Later when we talked on the phone, I told him we could go out again, but I was not having sex without an emotional connection first, no matter how long that took. I never heard from him again. I am grateful he went away, but it took me a full few days to allow that old turmoil to leave my system.

I really consider now when to share my sexual abuse. In releasing this book, I know I will need to do publicity about the subject. Yet, in writing through the journey of recovery, I see it is my awareness of what I get to uncover about the true me now that is the ultimate message.

WRITING PROMPT:

Have you trauma bonded with anyone romantically? How did that feel? What would be different if you held back and waited a few dates before you shared about your abuse?

I was contacted randomly on Facebook by a friend of a friend. He may have been flirting or networking but when I asked him why he contacted me, he said he felt an energy. I felt comfortable with attention in a non-addictive no high stakes way so I engaged in light banter. He had been in a few movies in the 90's, and I was a producer at that time. Then the conversation took a wide turn left.

He informed me his ex wife had poisoned his son against him.

"In what way?" I asked.

"She convinced him I touched him," he replied.

"Did you?" I asked.

"No, of course not," he replied.

The wind was knocked out of me. This was not a dynamic of abuse that I thought much about since my discovery of my own history of abuse. I reflected back on a friend of mine in Seattle who started dating a man (who became her husband) with two little kids. She was a wonderful attentive step mom, but the soon to be husband's ex wife did not like her. She created a story that my friend had "touched" her son while putting on his swimming trunks. She had not only told the father this, but had talked to her son about it, and then had almost convinced him it had happened. My friend stood her ground. She had not touched her stepson inappropriately. Period.

I was candid with this new Facebook friend. I told him that while it is sick for people to USE false abuse against children to mess with adult romantic relationships, his son would one day actually know the truth if he had been touched. Abuse survivors have an uncanny intuitive nature that we eventually can't ignore. I told him if his son's mother lied, one day the boy will know this as well, and he will hate his mother for it. I told him I was an abuse survivor which he was taken back about, yet wasn't that intuitively why he was telling me this story?

In this instance it felt relevant to reveal my abuse, from a place of experience. You will experiment with telling your secret. Sometimes you may be met with blank stares. Wrong audience. Just remember regardless how awkward, it is not for them. It is for you.

Despite my strong belief in the truth of the abuse, I did suffer various times in recovery with doubt. I even almost stopped writing this book because I felt guilt about calling out my dead dad publically. I called my AA sponsor teary.

"I don't know if I can finish this book. What if I am wrong?" I cried.

Luckily she has been with me the whole time as a witness to all my breakdowns and breakthroughs.

"Oh honey," she said to me. "It so happened. No way it didn't."

I was so glad to have her in my court. I continued writing the book.

WRITING PROMPT:

What does disbelief in your sexual abuse look like? Depict in writing the person you would be if you were lying. Then compare them to the loving image you have of you. What does that comparison feel like?

I can give you hope that one day, with the right mind set and belief system, your history as a sexual abuse survivor can help others 95% of the time. And when that 5% tries to make you put up a wall or protect the little girl in the bed, you have enough awareness to know it's going to be okay. It's done. Nobody is going to sexually abuse you again.

Chapter Seven
Taking Back your Body

For a lifetime, I treated my body with the same energy it had contained when under the control of the abuser. It was a foreign object to me. I had no connection to it. My body just did stuff. Little did I know it was acting out repressed dark inner secrets. I wasn't listening. I tried to say "No" but I was still conditioned to say, "Yes". As I healed from the abuse and added into my life a healthy component of wanting sex and intimacy as a single woman seeking a partnership for the second half of my adult life, I had to learn different reasons to say "Yes" to sharing my body. It was sometimes a simple sexual relationship with no strings attached and other times it was important to say "No" if I didn't feel spiritually centered in my body. I was not able to make these differentiations for a long time. It required a one year abstinence as well as some sexual exploration to find the balance.

For my whole life, my body was the vessel that carried my unshaped spirit, and it manifested disease and trauma to protect and loathe itself simultaneously. The body is as fascinating to me as the mind, and I never thought of them as interconnected because I had separated so severely. Before I faced the abuse, I was numb to my organic spirit-driven desires from the neck down. I was constantly in a battle to stay thin enough, limber enough, to be accepted by the world and to be loved sexually by a man attracted to me. I orgasmed plenty, danced sexy. I was long distance runner and a hot yoga practitioner but never for the benefit of my inner self. Even the running produced thinking time steeped in escapism. I ran and ran, fifteen miles at a time. I couldn't run from the truth no matter how much concrete my feet pounded. My ego was in a desperate race to keep the abuse repressed. I was willful and determined until the bitter end to accommodate my ego and not face the truth.

The abuse shame physically manifested when I was eighteen years old and living and working in Cape Cod for the summer with a best friend from college. We worked as waitresses and the rest of the time we were wild, drunk and free. I had a boyfriend at the time back in Rhode Island who had been only the second sex partner in my life, so even my version of sleeping around didn't add up to much compared to other teens we associated with on the Cape. That said, I had two one- night stands without protection (our generation was terrible with using condoms), and sure enough woke up with burning sores. I went straight to the emergency room in Hyannis. I was examined by a tired looking doctor. With not even a hint of emotion, and perhaps a little disgust on his face, he called it out as Herpes.

I was stunned. "That can't be possible," I said not finishing the sentence.

I'm not even a slut, I thought.

Then it hit me. I would have this for the rest of my life.

"I'll give you a minute to process this and I'll send a nurse in to discuss treatment," he said.

"Okay," I croaked. Treatment? I'd read about the big H. There was no treatment. It was contagious as fuck so I would have to tell everyone I slept with from that day forth that I had Herpes if I had an outbreak. I didn't even think for a moment how painful sex with an outbreak could be. There was no compassion for myself, or anger about one of those dudes giving me Herpes. It was locked in. I was damaged goods. It was affirmed. I was dirty and damaged. Instead of coming awake to sexual abuse at that age, I now had a more obvious secret I could "confess." Phew. Herpes allowed my sexual abuse to stay dormant because it took all the focus.

I told my first husband about my affliction before we started getting physical. It was the honorable thing to do.

"So I think you are great, and we are clearly attracted to each other, but I need to tell you something. I have Herpes."

In reflecting back now, I see it was a perfect set up for me to expose immediately how damaged and unlovable I was. If you take me with this scar of imperfection, then it means you really care about me. Therefore I'll take you no matter what even though I'll destroy you because I have worse secrets I won't face.

I went through decades of debilitating outbreaks. In the first inception of chat rooms, I joined Herpes Anonymous. I knew I needed support but it was so archaic, I never really had a community. I think back now to how the outbreaks happened and what they did for me. I used them to not engage sexually (obviously) with my first husband and my second husband. What is most astounding to realize though was when my dad came to town, they were worse. I recall one visit the sores hurt so much I was limping. I would do all the old fashioned remedies. I would sit on the toilet and cry, gauze pads soaked in witch hazel administering to the sores. Whole weekends saddened by this curse. Drinking gallons of raw cranberry juice and taking Lysine. I would be forced to ease up on alcohol but I would smoke pot to escape.

I even took special medication when my children were born should the Herpes flare up from the stress and the kids be born blinded by the open sores. I was tormented by the thought of scarring my children in vaginal birth, and so I was relieved when both babies were c-sections.

When I divorced my second husband, I went to a new ob/gyn. My original doctor had died and this new young doctor was his replacement. I walked in the room and immediately was attracted to him. I could feel his attraction to me as well. I should have left right then and there and found another gynecologist. But I didn't. Instead, I told him I was planning on dating and wanted to get the status of the Herpes in check. I hadn't had an outbreak in over five years (my dad had been dead for six) and I was feeling a sore down there. Could he check it out?

He looked at the sore and said it wasn't Herpes. He asked me aside from that original diagnosis in 1988, had I taken an actual blood test? I was baffled. A blood test? No, I had just assumed I had Herpes and then ran with it for the last two decades. I then started to think about how I never gave it to anyone. I was on the pill for most of my life so I didn't use condoms with my husbands. He administered the test and I waited.

The next day I got the news. I tested negative for Herpes.

I was blown away. I sobbed in the examination room. The doctor was even blown away. He couldn't imagine I had never gotten a second opinion. I had signed up for some bullshit branding at eighteen. That was part of my sexual abuse repression.

So I went right to my next best idea... I had brief torrid sexual affair with him. Of course I did! He was my angel! He had freed me with miraculous news, and therefore he should have my fresh and clean vagina first! Herpes free sex to celebrate! It didn't take much pushing to get him to oblige. All I had to do was agree to not be his patient anymore. At this point, I didn't give a shit. I was laser focused on having my first Herpes free sex with someone. This was the beginning of me heading to my sexual bottom. It was this bottom that contributed to me finally having the dream that forced me to face sexual abuse. It was this bottom that showed me how erratically I had gone off course in my life. Even for me who had always been a bit wild. I took pictures of myself in dressing rooms in lingerie and I masturbated and came in restaurant bathrooms and made videos and sent them to him. When I tired of him, I moved on to the next guy and did this behavior, and then the next guy. I am sure a close up shot of my vagina is someone's screensaver. My inner soul untreated from abuse headed to a dark bottom of despair. This sexual expression was not joyous and free. It was sad and lonely. I still didn't know how to cope with or celebrate the fact that my body was telling me something. I still wasn't listening. I was still treating it like some baggage I carried around on my back. I didn't celebrate not having Herpes with a day at the spa. My best idea was to get fucked as much as possible.

Luckily this phase was quick. As much as I wanted to act out, there was a reason deep down I had been monogamous in two marriages for two decades. I was still looking for love. My sad little girl was convinced at this point she would never find it, so she was using what she thought was her best attribute to survive: her vagina and her sexuality.

WRITING PROMPT:

What is your relationship today like with your sexuality? If it wrote you a letter, what voice would it have?

When I started therapy for sexual abuse, it hit me. The "Ghost Herpes" as I coined it was my body reacting to the sexual abuse. As soon as I got into a relationship with a man that showed signs of potential emotional intimacy, the Herpes flared to keep me safe by controlling what I could now; sex. Unlike in the abuse, as an adult I could say, "Oh, sorry, having an outbreak, can't have intimacy with you, stay away from me, I'm sick and damaged and I am going to isolate and nurse my wounded self in the corner." So on one hand it kept a deepening of intimacy at bay, but also protected me from a lifetime of promiscuity. Abuse survivors can take the direction of overt promiscuity. Aside from these bouts of being single and Herpes-free, that wasn't my story. These debilitating sores prevented that behavior, and in reflection, I am blown away by the capacity of my body to create a protection mechanism on so many levels for me, and yet for me to be completely so unaware. I couldn't see what was happening. I wrote the story I was sick, I was damaged, so I just hated myself and nursed my sores like a dutiful patient.

The outbreaks were especially intense when my dad would visit. I would tell him about them. I would limp around. He was mildly sympathetic. My body was making sure that mother fucker didn't lay a hand on me so it gave me the fiercest fire of defense.

Let me be perfectly clear here. There is no shame associated with having Herpes. I know that more than half the population is affected. I know people who live with it shame-free. BUT for me, it was an ailment that was not Herpes and the point here is that I made it something it wasn't to serve my bottom shelf self worth. I gave myself a sexual ailment I didn't have because I thought I was a sick, bad dirty girl.

WRITING PROMPT:

Write your health biography from the point of view of your body. Is there any ailment you have that you could explore the validity of further? Listen to your body tell you how it feels today. What does your body think of your strengths and weaknesses?

I soon manifested new physical ailments. My body violated from infancy had a lot of psychic and cellular programming to reverse. I was going to take my body back but first I had to reclaim it. After facing the abuse, I developed a constant nervous feeling in the back of my throat, like the acid reflux had met the anxiety and they were tap dancing on my esophagus. Nervous jittery twinges on my trachea. I then couldn't swallow food effectively. A normal piece of peanut butter toast with coffee needed four glasses of water to get each bite down. I was awfully perplexed by this condition, but chalked it up to anxiety and part of getting sober. Resistance to having a voice. I would share about these severe manifestations at AA meetings and women would nod. I realize now that while I absolutely love AA, it was not the right place to be vetting my health. I didn't seek any other counsel, started to limit what I could eat and I dropped weight.

The thin body image I had always maintained to be attractive to men, to me, and to feel like I had value was no longer something I had work for. My body was starving me. In a sick way, I liked how thin I got. I bought clothes again in the pre-teen section. I liked the attention. My boyfriend at the time liked my thin body. His prior girlfriend had been like 80 pounds, so I felt for him to truly love me and stay, I had to be thin. I did not love myself enough to take more significant action and seek medical assistance … I was good at keeping secrets about what is happening to my body. I would muscle through and the ailment will just go away

It was either out of fear or loyalty I did not tell what my perpetrator was doing to my body. Fear that the family would crumble, fear it would stop and I liked the attention, and perhaps a daily belief that it wasn't real and that I made it up in my head. This leads to an adult life of warped perception in all areas of your life. Did that happen or not? Maybe I shouldn't say anything because people will think I am an alarmist. At a young age I lost that intuitive validation of what is healthy to express for your own safety, security and happiness. My best adult course of action through my throat affliction was to intellectualize in my head. I am all alone and not with God (because where was he when my body was doing weird stuff as a little girl while being touched?).

WRITING PROMPT:

Are you efficient with your routine medical check ups, and if you don't feel well, do you believe you are valuable enough to get decent care? Write about the last time you were sick, and what relationship you had with your body in this time.

On top of it, I was a recovering addict. Addicts are actually very intellectual people. They can connect dots in their mind that lead them to incredible out there hypotheses that really are designed to hurt them in the long run. I was often my own therapist even though I had a therapist. So I also became my own medical practitioner. As the choking on food grew gradually worse, I believed it was in reaction to my experiences with children in the classrooms while substitute teaching. If I was teaching 3rd graders, for the first time I was flashed back to what it must have been like for me to go to school at eight knowing I was a sexual abuse victim. If I was teaching first grade, I would view these sweet innocent children understanding fully what it must have been like for me as a small child carrying the secrets of the abuse in my home to a day at school. One day I was teaching kindergarten and I choked so hard on a piece of bagel, I thought I was going to have to vomit into the trashcan in front of twenty-three little kids. This age of five appeared to be the epicenter of my trauma. No one to talk to or run to. My throat constricted shut and I was helpless, suspended in time. Luckily they were busily working on a craft project at their tables, so I desperately worked to get my throat to swallow the lodged bite of bagel. Tears welled up in my eyes and burned hot down my cheeks. Eventually, I burped up enough bile and coughed my throat raw to open the passage up. I was exhausted and scared. I thought, I don't think I can eat anymore. I was suddenly very sad for that little girl that sat in class knowing her dirty secret, knowing she was different. I wished so much I could travel back in time and speak up for her, and change what was happening.

WRITING PROMPT:

Are there any ailments you are currently have that prevent you from doing the basics like eating and sleeping? Create a character that has that ailment. What would you tell them to do?

Now my body was no longer getting the nutrients it required. It was impossible when all my throat would swallow a day was a Cliff bar and a fruit drink. A bad flu made its descent the day after I told my mom about the abuse. I was flat out in bed sick as a dog with a weird lump on my chin. I thought the lump was a really bad zit. I had repressed sexual abuse, false Herpes and alcoholism for decades. I wasn't going to be a kind master of my body. I let it go and it grew. I finally researched and found out it was an abscess. Other definitions were a boil or a carbuncle. In Louise Hay's book, You Can Heal Your Life, she attributes an abscess to "fermenting thoughts over hurts, slights, and revenge". A carbuncle is described as "poisonous anger about personal injustices". She also pinpoints ailments on the left side of the body as "representing receptivity, taking in, feminine energy, women, the mother." That was pretty mind blowing considering the conversation I had just had with my mom. I finally made a doctor's appointment when the pustule on my face was pounding. I walked into my doctor's office and she looked at me with grave concern.

"Oh God, Kim, you do not look good. What took you so long to come in?"

I looked at myself in the mirror from her response and saw what I had become; a gaunt thin woman with a huge bump on her chin. With abuse, there are not many ways to look at yourself in the mirror except, "Am I pretty enough to be objectified?" Or "I loathe myself so much I am going to pick at my face and scar it so I can be the damaged reflection I believe I am."

The abscess had turned into streptococcus that had spread into my blood stream and was slowly poisoning me. She did blood work and yes, in fact the abscess had spread bacteria into my bloodstream and it was attacking my body. I knew that this was indicative of the trauma oozing out. She prescribed me double antibiotics but more importantly I finally told my doctor about my trouble eating. She recommended a throat x-ray. I scheduled one and then cancelled it. My denial was so thick. I did not want to have any medical treatments. I had been opened up twice for a urethra stretching as a baby, I had two c-sections, and umbilical hernia after my second baby and then of course there was the invasive sexual abuse. I wasn't eager to trust anyone with my body. Despite really loving my general doctor, I was also scared I was dying right when I was finally getting my shit together.

I went to work the next day (substitute teaching) because I needed somewhere to go. I went to therapy and cried and screamed. On the way home I dictated into my Iphone a letter to my then- boyfriend about how dark my emotions were and how lost I felt about not knowing who I was anymore. I still couldn't hold those feelings for just me and God. I needed a guy to hear them. To validate the lost empty slate of my life. I told my body, assured it, that these secrets I had no longer needed to be contained deep in my body, and were being set free. These ailments were the final frontier of the toxic secrets of shame oozing out of me. The nastiness of the trauma in my body, deep in my cells wanted out.

Apparently what I was going through was too much for my boyfriend to handle.

He broke up with me three days later.

Him leaving was a miracle. I was too focused on being a perfect skinny girlfriend to save myself from sickness. I was in denial that I could not even swallow. I got fierce about healing my body. No weird ailment was going to hold me back from life again. I was taking charge. Ha. No, I did not call my doctor and get that x-ray. I decided I would learn how to live a productive life <u>on a liquid diet</u>. God was completely absent from this decision.

I researched the best way to get nutrients in your body with liquid. I devised a clever plan of self-will despite the fact that now I was waking up in the middle of the night throwing up all over myself. New restrictions were implemented. No eating after five o-clock. No more chocolate. I stopped exercising to keep up my calorie count in check. I had a friend come over and elevate my bed with bricks so if I slept at an angle my throat wouldn't burn while I slept. I became a connoisseur of pureed soups and veggie and fruit smoothies, and finally with my elevated bed I had four nights of amazing sleeps. I could live this way! I would still periodically Google acid reflux but there were aspects of that ailment that did not cover what I was experiencing. My thoughts would wander to throat cancer which kept me farther and father from getting real medical help.

I would pray to God for guidance but I was not listening to his answers. I was listening to me telling God what I wanted to hear. God was not interested in my plan. He was ready to take me to a higher place.

WRITING PROMPT:

What does your higher power, God, serving force, tell you about your life today? Can you tell the difference between your voice and a more spiritual loving voice? Write to yourself from you, and then write to yourself from God, and see the difference in how the two talk.

The next idea was to visit an intuitive healer. Chad Brown is a hulking figure with a booming voice and the gentlest deepest heart. He taught me tapping and told me I needed to look deep into my throat and find out what is down there. My old body, the trauma, the old ideas, would scream at me to stop investigating what is going on. They'd say, "We don't like this. You need to stay where you are, where you have been forever. You can go back to your ex husband where there is financial security, and you can drink again, and your family will be together again." Luckily, I knew just enough to face that this reality was gone and for a good reason.

Chad would touch points on my body and then stand across the room. I would twitch and release in the energy field. It was brilliant to feel the repression that was deeply imbedded start to wash away. One session, I saw the brightest light inside me. It radiated from my heart. I witnessed my capacity to be big and bold and beautiful. I was totally freaked out. I could tell the real me was trapped inside my body and wanted out. My true adult soul was held captive by a really pissed off revengeful scared little girl. I only did a few sessions with him, but he was an important road in this path to my freedom. He was my magical forest. My work with him gave me that next step to accepting I needed medical help.

First I had to get even more pissed off at God. Radically pissed. I was still in "Why me God" mode. I was operating on base level with God and my small dreams. I conceptualized a world that was only as big as my limited fragile thinking had allowed me to create. It was a dangerous, hard, slog through mud world. God was waiting for me to stop thinking small and get better so he could align with me and find the next path for my new life.

I entered a stage of low grade depression that I know was perfectly normal because there was a small part of me that knew enough about God and about recovery from sexual abuse that something better was around the corner. I needed to be open to it. To wake up and smile and feel confident in myself. I knew I didn't need depression medication. I had done that in my 20's and understood this was a different feeling. I forced myself to exercise and do the errands in the car, playing no love songs (an "I am alone" triggers) and while it wasn't a smiling joy ride, I got the day done. Chad had simplified my state of mind for me.

"If you are angry or you are tired you need to simply say, 'I am angry and tired today.'"

Stay in the moment was a new concept. A radical concept. My mind has always been one step ahead of where I am in all my affairs except when I write. Then I am right in the moment because I have a connection from my mind to my hands to the keys or a pen and paper. In reality, I could ping around like in a pin ball machine. The constant filling of spaces to 'carry on' wore down my nervous system. It eroded my soul. I didn't know how to be okay in just today and owning it and not making any apologies for it or fearing it. Part of getting authentic and having faith was knowing tomorrow will be a different day with new experiences on a variety of levels.

I worked with Chad a few more times. He taught me tapping for anxiety. It was calming to be with man who connected to me physically to heal me but we were not sexual. His healing helped me feel back into my body in an way that took the trauma and rewrote it. He worked with me to realign my body in a way that was new and completely free of the old constraints. I trusted him when I closed my eyes, laid on my couch, and he touched just the tops of my toes. While I tapped points on my body with him, I talked freely about my ex husband and the feelings I had about that ending. I had stuffed all that grief because I was so vigilant and angry. No matter what the end result was, as shitty as the ending years were of that marriage, divorce is a death and I had to grieve to move on. To believe I have the right to have that kind of support to heal, and to believe God will provide me the abundance I need to make sure I can have the support I need to heal is a profound belief that requires a lot of rigorous care to my connection to God.

Chad taught me what my truth was one day may not be my truth tomorrow. Stay open.

I made one more move before I went to the doctor. I had a private yoga lesson with super hot British yoga instructor. I told myself if I could do yoga in my very skinny body intimately with this guy alone for an hour without trying to flirt or coerce some kind of sexual connection, I was really in a far better place than I could have imagined. He was sweet and kind and I did my yoga and then he left. I wrote about it in my journal and then sat and thought about all these stages of dealing with my body. I looked at how small my thighs had become and my cheeks sunken in. I missed food and abundance and desperately in that moment knew, I wanted to finally love myself. I was done abusing myself. I didn't need to carry on the baton of my abuser anymore.

I went back to my doctor. She weighed me in at 105. I was 125 nine months prior; my weight my whole adult life.

"You are in a serious situation," she said. "I have a family friend who is a gastroenterologist. I am going to make a personal call to get you in to see him as soon as possible. This is serious. You may end up on a feeding tube."

I couldn't believe it and I was also so incredibly grateful to her and the gastroenterologist who diagnosed me from an endoscopy with Achalasia. When he called me with this diagnosis, I instantly cried.

"What the hell is that?" I said, tears pouring down my face.

"Well, it's a rare autoimmune disorder where your esophagus loses its motility."

"Why? Why now?" I said.

"There's no rhyme or reason for it," said the doctor. "It just happens to people your age."

In that call adult Kim took over for the scared little girl and told her the situation was going to be okay. We now had answers...and solutions.

I was no longer a victim. I was in charge of my body as a grown adult.

God gave me this ailment so I could take back my body as an adult from the frightening protective child in the corner who had lorded over it from day one that she had been violated. It took me the whole process of choking and gagging to get to that realization and own it. *The Devil screams the loudest right before he dies.* I turned away from the devil and towards God.

I had to endure an Esophageal manometry test to be on record with my health insurance that I in fact had Achalasia. They measure the lack of motility in your esophagus. My surgeon Dr. Chen revealed later that he never tells patients just how hideous this test is because no one will go. The technician administering the test said 50% of the people abort it in the middle and don't get the surgery approved. I am so proud I made it through, but man, was it an act of sheer will.

My friend Lynn joined me for the test because I have learned through my twelve-step recovery to not do anything alone. I am so glad she came. The technician put a four foot long metal tube that looked like something that should be hooked up to a carburetor up my nose, down my throat and into my stomach. There is no anesthetic administered because they need you alive and awake to swallow. They strapped it to my face and started to pour liquid down my throat. If you recall, I can't swallow food or liquids down at all so it just pooled in there and I gagged and choked and pounded my heels on the table and cried out for it to stop. Lynn said it took everything she had to stay in the room. It was unbearable to witness. Banana goo followed the water, and I choked and gagged on that substance for ten minutes. When it was done, as if from behind a magic curtain, one of the leading experts in the country for Achalasia, Dr. Jeffrey Conklin, appeared and confirmed I had Stage One Achalasia. I told him how little I ate, and how I was down to 105 pounds. He fast tracked me into a consultation with my surgeon and within two weeks I was being operated on.

I learned through this process that abuse survivors' great capacity to endure stress and trauma helps us manifest a bigger life. We can walk through more real life shit. We have a deeper capacity to stand strong in the face of adversity, fear or uncomfortable growth. This is one of our blessings from the abuse. I was scared for this test but I was strong. I knew this was part of taking back my life and I was not going to let any part of me quit.

WRITING PROMPT:

What medical treatments have you undergone since the abuse? Write about your experience in one and describe in vivid detail what you recall seeing and perceiving about the experience.

The Universe is profoundly interesting if you are open to healing on all levels. My mom insisted on coming to take care of me the week of the surgery. As a child I had been operated on not once, but twice under the age of two for a urethra that needed stretching for reasons unbeknownst to anyone in the medical community of this day and age. When I had asked my mom, "Why uretha stretching?" her reply was "That was what people did back then." She had been told I had an abnormal bladder and it needed to be stretched. Why a child at eighteen months and then again at two years old needs to be operated on for an abnormal bladder is beyond me, but I can't help but think it had to do with being abused. I had to bury my resentment at my mom for not just allowing that to happen, but that she was doing the best she could with the life she was in and the tools she had to cope.

I saw my mom's desire to come take care of me during the Achalasia surgery and hospital stay as her redemption for these heinous operations. I allowed her to come but I made a pact to myself that I was going to be open with everyone at the surgery. I was going to tell everyone when I was scared. I was going to cry if I needed to, and I was no longer going to be a quiet victim like that little child. Or a trooper like during my first c-section that happened after fifteen hours of failed labor. That mode was done. Waiting in the prep room for the anesthesiologist, I told my mom I was scared. I cried. She did the best she could to console me. She did not try and shut me down and she stuck it in there with me. It was not about her. It was about me revealing fully who I am. I am very sensitive to anesthesia, so when they gave me Dilaudid to just "mellow me out" before the big stuff, I passed out completely.

Later after the surgery my mom shared with me how my desire to no longer be silenced had manifested.

"While you were still deep under in the operating room," she said, "You sat up and started shrieking and yelling 'I'm scared, I'm scared!'"

"Really?" I said tickled pink at my commitment to self-expression in a time of great invasion.

"Yes," she said, shifting a bit uncomfortably in her chair. "None of the nurses knew what to do with you. Frankly, it was quite freaky."

"Well, I am sorry you had to experience that," I said (although I wasn't sorry at all). I sat back in my bed grinning from ear to ear. I had done exactly what I wanted. I had a goddamn voice. I had spoke up and spoke out and not given a shit what it looked like to anyone.

Recovery from the surgery was another trial in faith. The epidural they kept in me for three days really messed up my digestive system. I got a little manic with laxatives, buying everything Rite Aid sold, until a friend suggested I was acting addictive with them. Could I just chill out and trust? It had only been two weeks since the surgery. I fought here as an adult the concept that God was giving me a chance to consciously reclaim my body as mine. The women around me were holding me up so high and strong to do so. I was so scared I had lost control of my body again after going through so much to get it back both physically, mentally and spiritually. This was also a journey I was never able to consciously have as a little girl. My body was used for another adult's selfish pleasure and because I repressed that use, I never was able to consciously get it back. So I gave it away again and again to men and husbands and boyfriends.

A girlfriend in recovery guided me to an amazing colonic clinic and that practitioner Stephanie Kimura of Iyasu Colonics in Los Angeles guided me through two one hour sessions of release. It was beyond simply a colonic. As she massaged my arms and hands and as I released, she told me I was going to be able to have my body back but I needed to be a partner with it and not fight it. It was profoundly healing and eventually after a couple months, I started to have a regular experience with my body again. I had also almost immediately gained all the weight back, and was stunned to see how I was now the same weight as before the Achalasia, but just without the muscle tone I was accustomed to. Now God was really having me face my true body. Could I love myself a little fleshier and flabbier? I went through a period of anger and regret until I realized God had done for me what I couldn't do for myself. My body image was no longer what I used to be loved. I was not just a hot body anymore. I no longer was going to be defined by my body. I knew I still wanted to be fit and healthy, but I had other priorities in my life. I started to do hatha yoga, and stopped running as fast and as hard. I began to enjoy walks in the middle of the day for perspective and tension release instead of looking hot in jeans. Eventually, about a year later, I started to be in my body in a new way again.

I had to eat lighter as I would get full fast. The change was, I didn't see eating lighter as an opportunity to be uber thin by upping my workouts. I only did what felt right in my new recovered lifestyle. The body carries us around. We need to love it and honor it. Guys I would one day date needed to like the entire package I presented. Not just you're hot, let's have sex, and let's be monogamous because we are so fucking scared to live this life alone. No more actions at the expense of my ultimate soulful happiness.

I will admit I at first thought the choking manifested because I had been forced to perform fellatio on my father and it was a gag reflex, but there is no true memory of this, or flashback. Everything that happens to us in recovery does not align directly to the abuse. It was okay to have that thought for a moment, but it did me no good to mull over it. I just share it brutally honestly so if you have something involving choking, and you had that sickening thought, you are not alone.

Our adult selves can finally claim our bodies from our little children inside. They can finally rest assured we are going to take care of them now.

Chapter Eight
Generational Abuse: The Mad Mad Monster Inside

I walked through a dark seemingly never ending forest of abuse discovery to find that the first real love I could ever feel deep in my heart was for my children. I found myself at 46 years old, sober and frightened by how deep I was capable of loving. I went to my women's AA meeting and cried out of shame that I had missed my whole life not experiencing real love. How many friends and husbands and boyfriends had I experienced relationships with yet never truly had allowed them into my heart because my heart had been shut down from the abuse? Or never really met someone at a deep level of intimacy and trust because I frankly was not safe.

My bond with my children started to show itself in its power and intimacy because I opened my eyes to loving myself. Loving them and now some of the girlfriends in my life goes to depths that are still beyond my limited understanding. The feelings I have when I give my time and attention to them completely is so profound. I am proud of myself. I am finally living like a responsible healed adult parenting two children safely versus a terribly frightened tormented inner kid running the show.

Abuse when not dealt with trickles into all our affairs. Before I knew about and dealt with my sexual abuse, my sadness manifested into anger. I was always a fighter; with my dad, boyfriends, cab drivers, men on movie sets, anyone who didn't behave according to my standards. I beat up on computers and cars. I didn't know what was wrong with me. I knew I hated everything around me, and everything inside me, but pot and alcohol band aided my feelings on a temporary basis. My biggest shame that I had to walk through every day of my recovery until I stopped the behavior (and it does stop … I assure you, if you do the work), was when I hadn't corrected how I showed anger to my kids. It took my older daughter a year into my recovery to stop flinching if I moved too fast or to understand I was not being sarcastic. These were old tactics of domination and control that had been taught to me by my dad. It was not just the kids. I would discard people. I was cold to the humanness of others on a lower scale degree. I had no connection to self. How could I connect to you?

WRITING PROMPT:

How do you treat the people you love in your life? Your children? Your siblings? Your spouse. Do you yell? Do you understand why you are yelling? Write the words down about what you are yelling. Seek to understand.

Today I don't waste time with regret because on a continual basis my kids love and need me, and I am showing up like a rock star mom both logistically and emotionally. There are still days that I think about what it must have been like for my first born at five to look into my deadened eyes as I screamed in colorful rage. She was scared just like I feared my father. Or my mother finding out the secret. I would go into a fugue state as a parent and be not present. I was gone, and I would suddenly be in the mindset of the apathetic abuser. Soothed after being abused. After raging, I would provide comfort. I would swear my love and that next time she misbehaved, I would be kinder. I would be gentle. I had no God to pray to, and no one to talk to, so who was I telling all this to? While I did not sexually abuse anyone, I took on that same monster behavior of my sexual abuser. My angry abused sub conscious was in no way ready to change. I had no idea how futile it was. I actually thought my own will against a force I had no idea I was reckoning with (denial) could change something.

WRITING PROMPT:

I know this is brutally painful but if you have been abusive to your children as an unrecovered abuse survivor, you need to write about it and try to dislodge old patterning so you can cut the chord to the passing down of this behavior for future generations. Your shame is less important than the ceasing of the history.

When I lashed out on the kids or on my then-husband, I felt all powerful but I really had no power in my life. I had been rendered so powerless since infancy when the abuse began. I was clawing for some kind of truth that didn't exist. It made the little monster inside me, the inner child monster, angrier and angrier. It truly wasn't until my dad died, and I left the marriage, that I had the courage to start to wonder what was wrong with me. I don't suggest that anyone needs to clean house with their family to recover from sexual abuse, but that was how my story played out. The denial was so thick, and no journey had ever been mine alone, I had no choice to go it alone for the first time and really see the whole history. It had to be done for my children. Every time I grabbed my daughter's arm too tight, or pushed my little one because she wouldn't stop crying, I grew more and more in deep hate for myself. Once I was about two years into recovery from sexual abuse, and in counseling unspooling the acts of sexual abuse and the way that I had survived the world as a victim, I saw that I was simply re-enacting the monster that attacked me when I was little and helpless. The monster that silenced my voice. When my older daughter was little, I would silence her cries with a hand clamped over her mouth, even when it was a little too long and she gasped for breath. Or when she would not go to bed and I would scream and leave in a rage with a door slam. I am sure my daughter would shiver in her bed.

I would lose control of my capabilities to control the rage that grew inside me. I would love perspective of a smaller creature needing my love and protection. I was the monster that fed on me, and now I was feeding on my children. It is sad I didn't get it then. I had a repressed secret. I was angry and frustrated a lot. Thank God I also created lots of very happy memories with my children, but that does not make up for the screaming into their small faces. A switch would be flipped. I tried to tell some people. "Boy, I get real angry sometimes with my kids," and they would shake their heads and agree and sympathize and inside me was screaming, "No, you don't understand, the way I feel towards them is loathsome … can someone tell me to stop?"

In 2011 I had my first messenger. It was before I even knew or accepted I was sexually abused. I had just split up with my kids' father. I was so enraged and bitter and also at the time, completely over-sexualizing my feelings with any guy who would pay me any attention. I recall my seven year old daughter not wanting to get out of the car to go to a Buddhist chant on New Years Day (What kid would want to go?) and pulling her out of the car with such force, she smacked her forehead. I recalled not having any feeling about it at all. Later I thought, I am like a man who abuses his wife, cleans it up and then loves her again, and so she stays … but my kids don't have the choice to leave. They are stuck with me. I was so frightened and stunned by this thought. I had an Alanon sponsor and so I told her what happened. She was also in AA but I had not begun that journey.

She was the first person to ever say to me, "Kim, you are raging against your children and it is not okay. It could get worse. It is not acceptable and you have to stop today." I recalled the tone of her voice. It scared me. I knew she was right. I could not believe the monster I was becoming. I was so confused about how I had the capability to be a consistently safe, warm caring mother most of the time but then this monster would erupt. I made a pact right then and there to no longer lay a single finger on my kids or scream at them. For a little while, I did a lot better. There was an incident in the public library on a particular day where the tedium and monotony of 100% custody mixed with my lack of emotional stability caused me to think I had lost my phone in the library, and suddenly I went into a rageful tailspin. Screaming for my three year old to "Get out Get out" of the car. So fucking angry. I can't even believe today I would go to such frightening depths. I stormed into the library, swearing and yelling and found the phone, and drove home quivering in a simmering rage. If either child tried to talk to me, I told them I was so angry I couldn't even speak. They had done nothing wrong. If that happened today, oh man, I am so grateful to say it would be calm, serene, and frankly I don't really lose stuff anymore, and I surely don't blame them. I am raising two little girls to be bigger girls who love themselves. They feel the radiation today of my own self-love and assurance, my confidence and humor in my life. The taking back my life without it having to be a raging bitter act. I never picked the easy road in my life for change – I was always told I never used the back door but barreled through the locked front door. I began to behave better with my kids but as I had not come to terms with the abuse or my alcoholism, my heart had in no way unthawed. I was still the monster my dad had made me.

If this is happening to you, and you hate yourself for it, you can get well. I recovered and now my life with my children includes healthy boundaries and the love and communication is deep and honest.

I know there are mothers or fathers who are struggling with why they may manhandle their children and it is not evident yet that there was abuse in their past, or they know there is but don't believe that is why they are rough with their children. They think Inner Child work is a bunch of hooey. I talk about this in a later chapter, because I too was that "eye roll" lady any time anyone talked about their inner child work, but when I faced the fact that my inner little girl was repressed and was going to rage until she got the attention and acknowledgement to heal, I started to change my behavior in a radical way for the first time. My little girl was not going to allow me to give unconditional love to my complaining, consuming, joy-fully perfect little children until her complaints were heard from the past, and she was healed. She was going to use the unrealized unformed adult me as a vessel to minimize my children until her time in the sun was had. She was a terror and a tyrant.

WRITING PROMPT:

Have you identified your inner child? If you could for a moment play with that, what would she look like? What age would she be? What would she be saying to you, and what does she look like when she is really a mad mad monster.

I am absolutely not saying to you don't be angry or allow feelings to arise. Heck, more than periodically in this process you will be angry. You will feel an aversion to the very program or people who have helped get you to this point in your soul searching, healing from abuse and spiritual recovery. All I am saying is, maybe don't take it out on the little people who don't understand.

I live in my home now without a monster inside. My relationship with my daughters today is deep and wonderful and full of respect and love. My seven year old gives me long hugs and my pre-teen trusts when I don't accept her talking back I will handle it in a safe parenting manner. We do squabble and she slams doors and tells me to "Shut up" so I have to go into anger lock down mode. Seriously, any parent of a teen understands. Due to the yelling I did when she was little, my ten year old can't cope with me yelling at all. It used to send her into a two day trauma trigger. I did a lot of yelling because I couldn't hear my own mind, body and heart. I was dying inside. The abuse secret was eroding my soul and I was shouting to be heard. No one wanted to help me because they just wanted me to shut up and go away. I can yell around other people (a rare few) who can handle it, but my daughter is still too sensitive. Now we both understand more about each other and if we shout, it is a quick two minute yellathon where I need to get my own yelling in check first as the adult. I can accomplish this 86% of the time. Sure, sometimes you just want to lock your kids out of the house, put on Jazz music and make them go away until they chill the hell out. Yet, my capacity to cope and understand compassionately exists in my personality now. I don't blind rage. I may ramble on in an annoyed way, but it doesn't matter. My pre-teen tells me, *Talk to the hand, mom.* When we lie together in my bed and watch movies, and snuggle, it makes my eyes brim with tears in thankfulness to God for saving us. Helping me find freedom from the abuse and the courage to take these painful experiences and grow. To not perpetuate the hard angry inner child feelings anymore on my children. To love so deeply, sometimes I think I am just going to burst. Eventually that high of love gets mellowed out … not in a bad apathetic way, but it becomes your new norm, and it isn't another form of an addictive high that can burn out. You start to live for the first time in the gracious middle. Love is a steady stream with lowered expectations of others, but high consideration for myself. I can love with awareness and compassion instead of hole-filling expectation.

My pre teen will continue to test me, but the world is testing her all the time. She has called me a liar and a cheater. She gets into high anxiety if she thinks she can't pass a test, or complete a school project (she is an A student). Her little sister can fly into an insistent rage about being first in the bathtub or not finishing dinner. Sometimes they are both off the rails at the same time. In these moments like any healthy mom, a single mom (even though a lot of women who are married still deal with discipline alone), I take a time out in the bedroom and can easily get perspective back. I see it clear as a bell. I can't do any of my old behaviors at all anymore because they were so out of wack with how you treat people you love. I deeply love my children. I spend all the time I can with them. I don't trade time with them in for time with men I don't have a future with anymore, or drugs and alcohol. I don't rage at them. I pray to God that I caught my rageful behavior and stopped the family pattern soon enough.

If inside you there is a mad mad monster screaming to get out, and you hate yourself for what you do for others, I am here to confirm once again, it can stop. You can caress with those hands instead of repress.

I tell my inner little girl that I am going to take care of her and keep her safe. That I am an adult woman who has safety under control and can navigate the world not just so we survive, but so we have adventures and experiences beyond our wildest imaginations. Now that the secret of abuse is out, she and I can have that dialogue, a conversation that has developed immensely from the simple acknowledgement of the abuse, to conversations about the current life led that has nothing anymore to do with the abuse. We stop reacting to our adult life as victims and survivors, but instead participants in the present and the now with the new tools for living we are given in recovery.

Telling the secret is the key to releasing and reversing your inner Monster. The abuse in my house was a deep dark secret. My mom says she didn't know it happened at all. Today, even though a part of me wants to accuse her of looking the other way, I know my children love her and want to have a loving relationship with her as grandma. My AA sponsor explained that how I treat my mom is how I show my kids I want to be treated one day when I am grandma to their kids. Do I want them calling me each week and asking me to visit? Hell yes! So I need to show that example no matter what. If I get into the thinking of how my mom could not know, I get crazy in the head. Was she sleeping so deeply she didn't hear my dad leave the bed and go down the hall to my room? Where was she every night at bedtime when he would stroke my body parts to sleep? I could ponder so many variations of that story until the cows come home but it is the past and while I don't need to close the door on it, I don't need to piddle away the present obsessing over facts I will never know. When I cast the past accusations aside, my mom and I can have our own relationship and I discover she is a fun, loving supportive woman with a lot of life knowledge.

The big question is, why didn't I tell anyone ever? It was my special secret. My mad little secret. I held it close and tight and locked it away and made a resolve somewhere in my subconscious that no one would ever know. Until that was not possible any more ...

I won't let anything that happened in my life in cleaning up this dark wreckage be a secret. I am sorry that happened to my daughters. I am sorry that I emotionally beat up my first husband. I am sorry for the rage at my second husband. I am so grateful God helped me find a gentler and softer path. My relationship with all these people today is pretty darn amazing and respectful. I care deeply about all of them. If my children one day read this book and forgive me, even better. For today, if my ten year old has memories of something aggressive, I look her right in the face and say, "Yes, that happened and I am so sorry and it will never happen again."

WRITING PROMPT:

Have you raged on people in your life while you were repressing your abuse secret? How does that feel to you that I present the abuse in that way, as a "special secret." How does that land with you?

A woman in AA who had forty years of sobriety got a call from me recently. I was hysterical. Like a woman with a lot of recovery, she firmly got me out of the sobbing and into explaining what happened. I had seen a small glimpse of the old me in a fight with my younger daughter in the morning. She didn't want to go to school and was lying on the bathroom floor. I was yelling at her, and she was yelling at me. I was out of options, so I physically pulled her up by her shirt. The shirt sleeve left a mark on her arm, and she was plunged into despair of old man handling. I was devastated because I thought this chapter was closed in my life.

After my sober fellow calmed me down by getting me laughing about her own mishaps with her child, she told me this, "Kim, you don't want that life anymore. You know that. You don't have that life today. You are a sober wonderful mother. But you got scared. Do you want to be in sparring matches with your children?"

"No, not at all," I rasped out between sniffles.

"Then this is what you simply say calmly," she instructed me. "'There is no yelling at Mommie' and then you don't yell either. You tell your children that there will be no more yelling in the house. They can pound their pillows and scream outside, but not in the house. AND your daughter goes to school on time, or she is marked tardy."

I loved this advice. Now when either of my daughters scream at me, I calmly state, "There is no screaming at mommie." If my pre-teen rages on with I hate you and so forth, I keep repeating the mantra while also making sure she doesn't throw or break stuff. Finally I start to ask her what is making her so mad.

What happens now is a thing of sheer beauty. She admits she is sad.

She admits she is sad and she doesn't know what to do about the feelings because she doesn't know why they are there. I am able to get on the floor with her and hold her because I completely relate. I spent my whole life raging because of a locked away sadness I was not allowed to feel when I was her age. I had a dark secret and no one to tell and no one to hold me. I was an angry little monster.

I told her that when we don't talk about our sad feelings, they can manifest into anger, and that was happening for her. I asked her what the sadness felt like and she said it was like when you are going to sneeze but you can't and you hold it back and it just waits there. It was like that in the pit of her stomach. I held her as she let out a few sobs and then it was over.

I never believed I could love my children as deeply as I do. I never imagined I would learn to love them this deeply while having to share them in 50/50 custody. I have some deep healing to do, and when I am away from them, I continue to heal and fill myself with good messages, recovery, God, exercise, trauma release, writing and fun with girlfriends. I don't care about making a million dollars or marrying my soul mate when I'm doing the true inner healing. Holding healthy safe emotional space for my children are some of the best moments of my life. This shows me lives can be healed. This is a thriving family. I am no longer a monster.

WRITING PROMPT:
Destroy something in your writing. Just get out the literary hammer and smash it to bits. Let out all the glee and revelry of destruction.

Know that this is on paper and not harming anyone, or any property. You do not have to feel shame for your anger. You just need to smash and rage with words. When you are done, rip out the paper and put it on the floor. Stamp it. Smash it. Tell it you are done with rage.

If you don't have children of your own, do the following writing prompts to the children of friends you may know or be exposed to. You can also observe children at a playground or in a public place.

1. Free write about what it feels like to be kind to your children. If you don't have children, do you avoid children? Where do you find you get hard with them or freeze up your love, your playful nature? What are your limits? Push through and practice alternate behavior and write about how vulnerable it feels.

2. Make notes of little miracles that happen with your children/other young children. Can you tap into their young self? Be in wonder about their youth, innocence, and existing with no burden of the hardships of life. You can borrow their energy and wonder since you had yours taken away.

3. Write about what it would have been like for you as a child if you were looked at like a precious miracle? Feel those feelings and then give yourself that consideration.

Chapter Nine
Balancing Masculine and Feminine Energy

My whole life I was completely shut off from my female energy. The way I needed to survive in my life was in a very take-charge mentality with all masculine components. While I still am head of a household with two kids as a single parent, there are many sides of old masculine energy I happily let go of to let the woman inside me finally blossom and breathe. To be courted, and to enjoy pretty things. To be emotional at the drop of a hat but in a gentle nurturing way to myself. To take time to breathe and sit and meditate. To be caressed in a way that is a female woman, not a child. The feminine energy I needed to find, the woman that had been buried from developing for so long, was not just in looking hot! It is a feminine and masculine balance in my body.

Maybe you are confused reading this. You don't yet know what the hell I am talking about. When you are abused, you have your feminine and masculine power taken away simultaneously. The female side abused and the masculine too weak to fight. Feminine power is a hot topic these days. How we stand in it, how we dress for it, how we speak it without being too masculine. How to be feminine and still be powerful and what does that power mean? Sure, we all love a good estrogen filled fist pumping women's empowerment conference to tap into our feminine power, but that is not the work we are doing here. We are untangling from a perpetrator who became our emotional captor. Some women have power and have learned how to be feminine about it. I have always wanted to know their secret. If you listen closely to people in the limelight who came forward about their abuse, like Oprah, she has done a whole heap load of reading. It isn't all on feminine and masculine, but it is on the soul. In our soul lies both sides and they are both beautiful.

WRITING PROMPT:

What is the most prevalent energy in you currently? Masculine or feminine? Where do those energies preside in your life?

I was groomed to be a provider by the abuse, and a survivor, and therefore my masculine energy outside was a real pissed off little girl. Think a very young Drew Barrymoore in the movie *Fire Starter*. I took male roles in relationships where I was the one always on the man about how we didn't have enough sex (this was my worth). Intimacy with women friends in my twenties was one big party and doing drugs in the clubs (I'm so fun!). I didn't do self-care in a way that was innately feminine which included feeling soft feelings or shaping who I was as a woman who could take it easy, be provided for or allow my creative side to naturally evolve. I knew at twenty-five I felt old inside and already around the block yet I couldn't stop driving forward. I was cultivating the capacity for a deeper anger and hardness that would not start to be revealed until my second marriage, progressive alcoholism, and having children. I would try and get facials every six weeks to be female but I would spend the whole time complaining to her about my husband. I felt like I deserved these skin products and facials because damn it, I was a woman. But I didn't feel like a woman. I don't think I even thought like a woman.

I was powerless but not in a good way. I didn't like being powerless. I had not found the concept of powerlessness with God in twelve steps. I knew nothing of surrender to a Higher Power. Surrender was death. Hold on tight and it will be over, then hold on tight until it starts again, and then hold on tight until it is over. This was the cycle of my youth punctuated with drugs, alcohol, swooning over boys and that was about it.

Pregnancy for me was the exception. It was my most womanly time. I gestated two beautiful babies inside my womb. This was my female project. They were in my home. It was my power of creation. I wish that I had laid back even more to have joy in that process but I felt the gnawing agony of incompletion once they stopped breast feeding. Pregnancy was a beautiful time because my joy was inside me. Almost a decade later I saw I needed to heal my womb and my inner feminine core. My first delivery was a mess. After fifteen hours of a faulty cervix, they drugged me up more, cut me open and a baby was taken out. I never honored the fact that I went through extensive bodily invasion on my first child. I had so many drugs in me. I didn't even meet her or nurse her until five hours after the birth.

The next baby, my youngest, was a scheduled c-section. I was taking no emotional or physical risks. I had a well- calculated plan with a team of doctors. I had my baby in less than five minutes. I was able to be with her and nurse her on the spot. My one really feminine experience I had made efficient and effective.

A few years ago before I accepted sexual abuse, I was driving a friend and I to a hike. She had been one of the first women I had experienced long deep conversations with about emotions. She had also run on a high octane masculine energy for a long time too, at one time a high six figure bread winner for her family and then cheated on by her husband. She had her own baggage and crisis she was walking through, but we were both creative kindred spirits. In that car that day I had a moment that I knew I had been having since I was a little girl. I felt manly in her presence. My features felt masculine. I almost morphed into my dad on some level. She was feminine and I was the guy. It scared the shit out of me. I remember thinking, what is this? She was about a year ahead of me in coming to terms with her hard driving life crashing down to rise up again in a feminine spirit. I was seeing me in the lag behind. While she was far from fully formed herself, I saw what the next step was to freedom and femininity. Liking who you were no matter how your life is crashing down.

When I entered Alcoholics Anonymous, I went to women's meetings. I started to listen to, watch and learn from the women in AA. I shared about clothing phobias and sex issues, ex husband stuff, and slowly I started to feel love form in my heart like I had never felt before. I cried openly about how scared I was at my capacity to love my children. I also was terrified by my resentments, my judgments and my ability to use people to perpetuate my old story. Disheveled and raw, these women would listen to me and love me. I would observe the women wearing nice clothes with their hair done and their makeup pretty, and I would want to be able to access their ease, joy and grace. They healed my long dormant female insides by simply holding me in a strong loving space, and setting an example of stepping into their skin.

I never felt aligned with dressing pretty just for the sake of celebrating me. I was so shut down inside from my core self, everything was a cover of some kind. I was dressing up the sick lost little girl who never from day one was allowed to be an individual. I was a part of someone else. In the heart of my sex and love addiction, I migrated towards lingerie stores. Dress up feminine. It was again, another façade. I needed a man to tell me I was feminine by his raw desire for me. There was no real love in the equation. I was far at this point from sex and love able to hold safe space in a romantic relationship.

WRITING PROMPT:

Where would you like to better explore your feminine or masculine side? Have you been in autopilot in the way you dress or behave for the opposite sex to be seen as desirable?

When I started dating, I borrowed a few dresses from my sponsor because I had nothing that was pretty, flouncy and feminine. I surprised myself with my hair golden and curled, and my little dress and earrings, looking as feminine as I could. When that date saw me, I kid you not, a ray of sunshine lit me up, and a breeze ruffled through my hair. I could feel him witnessing my feminine beauty and being moved profoundly by it. Yet, it was still in the eyes of a man. How would I see myself as feminine for me? I finally decided I can't do this alone. I hired a stylist, and told her I hated shopping and was petrified of dressing the real me. She was so lovely. She went out and found me some clothes. She rearranged my very sparse closet, and she gave me permission to look at interesting clothes. She asked me to think about jewelry and desire a wardrobe as a woman. She helped me organize that side of feminine. To want to go out the door looking nice because it makes me feel good. To be seen fully in all areas of my life. My daughters even noticed when I dressed nice.

Being entrepreneurial can be very masculine. Running movie sets I was very masculine. Day done, now let's go boys … to the bar! Now running a business as a book coach, I enjoy a life balance with a lot of feminine. It turned my direction into being a healer with words, not a driver of words. Forty years one way, no identity, and you aren't going to ease into an absolute authentic feminine grace at the snap of a finger. I still have not made my house or my bedroom ultimately as feminine, or artsy or cool as I would like, but every day my vision grows. Even writing can be shared and expressed in a feminine/masculine balance. What used to be painful isolated survival starts to become genuine living.

WRITING PROMPT:

What areas of your life can you ask for help? Are there women who provide services that you can employ so you don't have to figure everything out on your own?

I don't need to bring more alpha male into the world in business. I can explore and present my talents in storytelling in a kind, firm insightful way. My clients need my intuitive gifts of storytelling, but they also need me to hold gentle space for them as they unfold their fraught pasts in their own version of repression. When I lose faith and worry about the future, I am not thinking as a woman who believes everything is bountiful and there for me, but as a man who worries every day about money. In my womanhood, I believe there can be ten minutes of not doing and just sitting in my glowing inner beauty to ask what is next. When I don't have contentment in myself, the creases in my brow furrow deeper. I am the trauma victim trapped in a masculine track that sees no beauty in the daily spill of life. In my feminine, I embrace my role as facilitator to blossoming souls. I can help people say in their most balanced sane way, what's next, world?

WRITING PROMPT:

Recall the last time you spent ten minutes doing nothing but allowing yourself to sit in the magnificence of your feminine grace. Write down how you feel in those ten minutes and do this exercise several times in a week. See what manifests.

One morning that masculine uncomfortable feeling I described in the car with my friend to the hike arose again as I worked at my desk. I was now radically self aware of the masculine trauma energy trying to seep back in. I went to an AA spirituality meeting. It was not a coincidence that I was the only gal in the meeting of about 15 assorted men. God is funny. He wants me to see I am not a man, but that I can be vulnerable with men in my own feminine power. This meeting was healing because I shared openly about this masculine energy that overtakes me and I didn't want it. I wanted to be free of it. The men heard me and I felt a layer of unnecessary masculine self leave. None of them wanted sex from me, and I wasn't impressing anyone. I never felt that pervading masculine energy again after that day. While sometimes I feel big in my body like a guy, I am more feminine than ever. The irony I see now is that feminine intuitive energy actually keeps me safer than masculine because it draws to me people who are in alignment with my soul energy. When I am in the masculine, I attract unhealthy power hungry people because that is not truly where my heart is centered as a mother, an intuitive and a coach.

I started to reexamine my personal definition of a female body. How comfortable could I be with a little stomach or a wider butt? What if I surrendered a lifetime mission to be lean, hot and tight for happiness? I struggled hard with fear of what my real body looked like, but my busy schedule led me to more organic exercises that took the focus away from being an object of external validation. I found I liked hatha yoga, walking, dancing with my kids in the living room. I didn't work out to "make me hot" anymore because that was connected to the old masculine energy. I enjoyed getting up from my desk and wandering about in the hills in the middle of a day. Working out grew into a fluidity of feminine and I never got fat. I just grew into my real beauty and softened, outside and in.

WRITING PROMPT:
What is your definition of a female body? What would happen for you if you surrendered your life quest to fight the body that was violated and allow it to flower and open?

In order to align myself to my feminine, I was abstinent for a year. I pretty much white knuckled it, but it had to be done. To find my feminine side, I needed to be man-free. Every single one of my female friends thought it was a great idea. They didn't even know the truth; that in all my interactions with women I couldn't shake the feeling that I was not like them at all. I was rigid and uncomfortable and I desired lightness and freedom. Sometimes in my socialization with women, I almost felt like I was preying on them because I was such an outsider to my femininity. For a brief spell I thought I was gay but I was not sexually attracted to women. I was definitely attracted to men.

I just wanted desperately to feel feminine.

Crazy thoughts went through my mind in my abstinent period like what if I get so anorexic developing new sexual values until I have met "the one" that I never have sex again? The sex I always had was to lock a guy in to a relationship. I hadn't ventured into one-night stands to meet my needs. When I finally did after the abstinent period, it contributed nicely to finding my feminine. It also helped me to hold off on sex with a man who I could start to sense was relationship material. I could hold off and see if they cherished me first. I wanted to be the woman who was oblivious a man loves her so much he watches her every time she goes in and out of a room or makes efforts to sit close to her. I was too focused on the lock down. The masculine conquest. He likes me, I like him, we better lock this in and jump right into courtship because frankly, I had no idea what courtship was. It had never been taught to me. So I started to ask feminine women lots of questions about being with men. I thought for a while I was all of their opinions instead of me. Then all of a sudden I gathered a new form of confidence. I could date and learn what I liked and how I liked it. I could say "no thank you" and not lose sleep.

After the abstinent period, I was wiser about how to approach relationships with men. Yet, I still had to go on too many dates with men with red flags. I was so smitten about my new-found feminine, I hadn't built the next muscle of discernment which was aligned with good values. I remember the first kiss with a guy I believed was good and safe. It felt like a drug. I wandered around my house in somewhat of a daze afterwards. I got obsessive about what this meant and what he thought and where this will go. I started to create a home with him. You know, that crazy woman thinking. Then I thought, shit, I'm not going down this rabbit hole again. I created a new mantra. 'He is just a nice man who likes me.'

I said it over and over and then turned the outcome over to God. He is just a nice man who thinks I am a sexy woman. In fact, he may think I have it all. Yet it is not my career driving and my sexual prowess that attracts him. It is my ability to show up and be feminine, move slow, communicate and be honest. Even the third or fourth date in with a man, I had not mentioned I was sexually abused. I didn't need to earn those stripes. I didn't need to share my trauma with a man until I felt we were in for a longer haul. Each experience taught me a course correction, and I went back to the mat. I wanted love as a woman. Someone to bring value into my life with my kids. The real me came out from the wood paneling, and she had a vision of her romantic future that was tangible but not attained without effort.

Today, I am on the path of a woman who loves her femininity. On occasional days femininity is profoundly awkward but when my feminine energy is balanced, my days feel glorious, vulnerable and empowering.

WRITING PROMPT:

Have you had abstinence from dating or sex for any period of time? Are you the aggressor in sexuality in your relationship or in dating? What do you think would happen if you did the opposite? Write out what the opposite of your sexual self would look like in a fantasy. Don't judge or hold back. Let your imagination rip and tell yourself it's okay to explore the inner feminine and masculine of sexuality.

I stopped sleeping with people I was dating. This was a challenge because ultimately in the back of my mind the end goal was sex. I dated a man two times, and on a third date we went on a lovely day to the beach. He brought his camera and wanted to take pictures of me. I had bought a nice bikini for the day and was feeling sexy and free. He had so far been a gentleman and so I was feeling safe.

"Go into the ocean," he said to me. I had been threatening to ride the waves all day. The surf was rough but I am an excellent swimmer. He wasn't a swimmer. He said the ocean made him allergic.

"Okay, I will," I said, and I strode into the ocean. I knew he would take pictures of me. I liked the attention. I body surfed a few waves, and there was a strong undertow. On my way out, I miscalculated a wave and it clobbered me from behind. The next thing I knew I was in trouble. I couldn't catch my breath and I couldn't find the surface of the water. I was tossed around and around with mouthfuls of sand and ocean water. I was thinking to myself, even for me, this is bad. I am frightened.

When I finally pulled out of it, my suit was off my breasts, sand was everywhere and I looked at him. He was still lying on the blanket. I thought, surely he had seen me almost drown. I came back to the blanket.

"Did you see that?" I asked him, trying to be casual about his clear ambivalence to my safety. I was fearful if I was too upset he wasn't concerned for me that I would be causing a scene and he would leave me. He would not date me again. I wouldn't get sex.

"Yes," he said smiling. "I got some nice pictures."

I should've dumped him right then and there but fear and shame for me with men is very strong from the abuse. I don't believe I have the right to speak up because I will lose someone and then feel ashamed I screwed up.

It's not surprising that the way this relationship unfolded over the next few months was of me feeling less and less safe and well treated. Red flags were waving and I ignored them. There was some questionable sexual safety. It seemed we were exclusive but it hadn't been properly discussed. I let jealousy make me crazy and I looked up his OK Cupid account. It was not only still active but there were new pictures and he was listed as single. I had mentioned to him kiddingly in the past that he looked far better in person than his profile and he should change some of the pictures. Now here he was, updated profile, talking about all the hiking and biking he loves to do that we never did. I felt my heart pound and race. It's like I lost consciousness. I had been lied to, deceived, my trust breached – confidently without any counsel with others, or a brisk walk of perspective around the block, I hammered out a snide bitchy text about how great his new pics look on the dating profile and how he can basically kiss my ass. He was indignant, and his explanation that a stalker ex-girlfriend updated his site, I actually felt like a jerk. I felt shame I snooped. Shame I didn't ask the right questions in the beginning or before sex. Shame I had sex without a commitment and now had no leverage because I was hooked. Out of jealousy and fear I acted like a crazy person and now felt ashamed.

I told every woman that came in my path that week about finding his active dating site. I still was not completely secure in my own heart's message. I needed them to tell me that it was not cool and I should dump him. I was looking for justification for my outburst and jealousy. The truth is, I didn't need to feel shame for my actions, but I can honor and respect myself to a higher degree and attract a higher caliber of man. It is not until I was so whole and happy with myself that I was able to break up with this person calmly and compassionately after a few more incidents of not being treated very well. I stayed in the basic principals of my values and desires for safety.

I am very grateful for this relationship. I learned so much about myself, and about men. He was a teacher who came into my life so I could humbly learn about shame and fear with men.

In order to clean up my relationship with the male gender, I had to forgive myself truly for my past sexual acting out behavior. I had to put the shame to rest. You can't be in your feminine with regret. A wonderful prayer, the Lay Aside Prayer, suggests you lay aside everything you think you know about an area of your life. I had to lay down all the impressions of myself like "I am just wildly sexual" or "I will never find a man who absolutely adores me." I had to accept I may know nothing about the male race despite multiple marriages and relationships. I had been on the same autopilot, just different man, different town, but same me. I had to lay aside everything I thought I knew and ask God for help show me how to be compassionate, friendly and in self-worth without wanting anything in return from the male race. My old fearful way of thinking about intimacy with men was not going to ever help me find a true life-long romantic partnership because I didn't think I was enough to demand a certain level of treatment. I started practicing first with my ex husband and also some of the men in one of my AA meetings. I learned how to be honest without rage or insult and have integrity but not use them to make me feel real, pretty, validated or whole. It cracks me up now that I talk to women who are having issues with men, and they think they did something terrible or said something terrible. I give funny candid advice like, "They are men, they have already forgotten. They just want to be treated nice. Just be nicer next time." I was never able to have that appreciation for men. I prayed on them to lure them in and then punish both of us for what my dad and I engaged in. I don't think they ever knew what hit them. I was a beautiful fun shit storm.

Socializing with the women in my circles of recovery because I wanted to, not because they were man filler or a professional connection increased my connection to my feminine during this period of learning about men. I was with women enjoying being a woman. I had to accept that sometimes they didn't like something I said, or I experienced old feelings from my teen years of being left out, or not good enough to be invited somewhere. Just like with men, instead of feeling shame, I accepted that they are human and have their own stuff they are experiencing. Unless it is a huge affront or insult, do I really need to blame people who do show love to me because I am in fear? I started to be open to asking them how they were, and calling women just to check on them. Go to the movies or take a walk with a friend. Have coffee with my sponsor in AA.

Even the relationship with my AA sponsor was a new female relationship I had not had for a long time, if not ever. She listened to me and I listened to her. Nothing I could do or say shocked her. She held me up as wonderful and powerful in the eyes of my God. We started to have very deep funny conversations. She did my hair. I started to feel what it was like to really be a woman. Not a damaged abused little girl who looked in from the outside at other women being healthy and not abused. I wasn't spilling all out and messy and with holes. I mean sure, I would break down, but for the first time I started to do it as a whole woman. I actually started to really love that I could cry. I love that movie with Cameron Diaz, *The Holiday*, where she can't cry. She tries and tries to cry and dates a man who can easily cry. At the end of the movie, she finally cries and it is a huge turning point for her. I always cried but it was because some man or career was ruining my life. I needed to leave that behind. My dad was long dead and the abuse was long over. I had new feelings to express, or to understand why I was not expressing them as the full woman I am today.

My path to understanding my feminine may be life long. I started so late in life. Yet I have a commitment to love. I met a man recently who is absolutely wonderful. I accept him for who he is. He thinks I am magnificent because I am independent, secure, but I am also honest about who I am currently in my life. I see a bright future for us, and I attest that gift to the writing in this book; the sharing and finding permission to be my fullest unapologetic resolved feminine self. Today there are very few rough edges to my feminine self. When they reveal themselves, I hunker down and do some more work. I will never be less than I was before.

Chapter Ten
The Inner Child's Voice

My inner child was not part of my concern. Ever. I was resistant and judgmental of the people who would speak about taking care of their inner child. Big eye roll to the folks who had actually named their inner child. I had enough trouble tackling maturity as an adult in the real world with two living breathing real children, never mind adding an interior child with demons to wrestle. No inner child discussion for me.

As a child, I was taught I had few needs. I was used. I was a vessel for pleasure and therefore my ultimate value as a child was to provide comfort and support to a man who was supposed to be protecting me. Having no self, I was a hollow shell of a little monster that grew into a big adult child who had the capacity to be a predator of others whether it was my children, men or myself. This was a bitter pill to swallow in the last few years and I knew that I could do the work to make it less painful, but I did not understand that I had to spend time healing the child within. My inner child was sitting on a stool in the corner covered in sticky chocolate, a soiled dress, her plump arms defiantly crossed over her chest, refusing to set me free until I listened to her, heard her voice. Instead I pushed any validation of her away, and projected her rough rawness onto all kinds of people so at least I had the power to make the choice to stay alone in a scary space. I'll piss on you before you piss on me, mother fucker, still had a voice even through the first year of abuse recovery. I had no idea how to ask for what I needed because I didn't know and no one taught me when I was young what to ask for. I was a pissed off neglected kid in a adult woman's body who didn't even know what it was like to be a woman.

WRITING PROMPT:

Are you resistant to the concept of the inner child? Write about why and what it would feel like if you took a leap of faith and wrote about the child that is within you. What would she or he want to say?

I would hear women talk in recovery meetings about their dirty shame. Because of the abuse, they couldn't feel their own bodies and would scream relentlessly at their children and their partners. They had terrible tantrums at work. The louder they screamed, the less people heard them and the more damage they did themselves and others. I was a raging dramatic screamer. I would tell my ex-husband I hated him. I would tell him he was an asshole, a fuck head. My dad would tell me I was an asshole growing up. While the words stung, it was his lack of remorse or apology that caused the most damage. Parents are human. We have breaking points. I would never ever call my kids assholes but I have had moments were I have gone off on critical tangents. I have made amends after without blaming them. Mommie shouldn't have said those things and she is sorry. Children are incredibly forgiving.

If the swear words and insults against others were translated, they would say, "You will never find the real me in here because it is a lost little girl." Your screaming won't stop until you address that little person in you that is screaming to get out.

When I started to release the shame of my abuse secret about a year into sobriety from alcohol, I softened and realized I wasn't as angry as I thought I was. I was actually a nice person. People truly liked me. A real seminal moment in my life was when my Alanon sponsor, not as a program suggestion, but as a friend and a fellow creative, suggested that I write to five people I had worked with recently and ask them a few questions about what they found to be my strongest assets. I was in tears as they described me as "friendly and 'the good guy'," "got stuff done without being a tyrant", "compassionate", " likable". I saw that I was changing. I was aligning with a core underdeveloped person deep underneath. My perception of myself was so radically different than what others observed in me. I saw a dark loathsome inner me. People saw a lovely hard-working woman with a fun spirit.

WRITING PROMPT:

Ask five people who have worked with you recently in some capacity to fill out a short questionnaire about your personality. Absorb what their perception is of you and ask why you can't see the positive attributes they see.

It is hard to love children when the child within you was so destroyed. If you don't know the child within you was damaged, manipulated and abused, then you really don't know why you want to hurt creatures that are vulnerable. You should love them, you think, as you rage at your child, or beat your dog. Your rage is blinding. You can't see through the red rage. How can you be compassionate if you were told to be quiet and take a violation that was done to you and not tell anyone? My dad use to say, "I'm so mad I see red." That scared me but taught me that behavior. If my children see me like that, they will take on the pattern. So regardless of whether my inner child feels a lack of compassion for my children, I had to love myself enough to teach her. I had to stop the pattern of abuse. I had to unconditionally love my children in a different way than I was loved, and my inner child needed to be shown I was in charge.

As I started to become more in touch with God, and work through the abuse trauma and gain more sobriety time, I faced the painful disconnection to my children when they were very little. Amid the truth that I had been a fantastic loving mom 96% of the time, the 4% was murky. I remember the splitting and disassociation I would feel at moments when they would cry for too long. I was cold as stone, and I wanted to crawl out of my skin, out of my life. Their unhindered emotion tapped that raw inner child that had not been allowed to openly express feelings. My inner child viewed my children as loud and naughty. "You need to squash them!" she would say. "They are insolent! You were not allowed that. Cork it now!" I would completely detach emotionally and that must have been so frightening for my children. It was like the abuse. You are lying there and you don't want it to happen, and you are being hurt or stuff is being done to you that doesn't feel intuitively right yet you look into the face of the assailant, my father, and he is shut off, detached, not there and you can't get through and yet you are powerless and helpless. When I watch videos of my small children, it is very painful even today. I can't bring back the first few years I was checked out of my youngest daughter's life with drinking and obsessing over men and disconnection to feelings, but I hope one day I can look back at their little lives and feel the joy that I finally know now in loving them fully and completely. I am too recovered now to behave any other way anymore. They are still children and I have the present day with them. I have time. I do my best to make that a very conscious part of my existence. I don't disassociate anymore. It used to destroy me when they would go with their dad because I had so much guilt and lost time. Now, it grows a bit easier as I stop beating myself up about the divorce and the past. I know when I am with them, they are safe and I am present. My inner little girl is calming down.

Disassociating with men was a favorite ploy of my inner child because she was never given an innocent childhood. My inner child was searching for the answers to the questions: Who are men? Why do we like them and fear them at the same time? I inform my inner child that as an adult, I can handle learning about men in a different way than my dad taught me.

At the start of my recovery, the framework of the abuse was it was done to me. It was the most painful unresolved piece. Something selfish at the hands of my male provider buried the forming child self, loved and created by God. I turned my tear-stained cheeks away from God. He did this, I thought. The curious little girl became a false self that was cunning, manipulative, angry, sexual and violent as protection against God. She didn't have a spiritual chance. It was like that movie *Poltergeist*. My inner child went into an alternate universe and came out a monster. She was manifested from an incestuous evil repetitive act. She was a little monster who wanted to do harm to herself and people she loved, then hate herself for it. She wanted to stop but couldn't stop and there are people who wanted to love her and know her but she couldn't take it.

WRITING PROMPT:

In intimacy with others, do you feel like an adult or a child? Is there a shame related to asking for what you want? Write about what it would feel like if you could explore your free self, born with the gift given to every man and woman of personal expression.

I had to take a strong hold of my inner child at some point and tell her, look, we can love ourselves. The madness can't go on. We are going to love ourselves if it is all we can do for a while. God loves us. When I realized that God did not do the abuse to me, a human did, and that was a human who had lost their spiritual path, I saw that God had actually saved me from any worse harm. God knew I would go on in life a warrior, find my voice, and write this book to help millions of people who didn't know the way through pain was with pen and the words. I sobbed a lot in opening up my inner child to fun and whimsy. I told her it was okay to remember the bad monsters spawned by evil. They have no God. We have God. Now I see that my message is one I can bring to other men and women who feel robbed of their childhoods and the natural inner child progression. Getting onto the spiritual path first is key before you can re-claim the inner child relationship.

Sexual fantasy and romantic delusion replaced the innocent imagination taken away by the abuse. I convinced myself in my late teens that I was a very sexual being, I needed lots of hard fast and intense sex. I didn't feel in sex. I would read in the sex abuse books about women who became really promiscuous due to their sexual abuse. That was not my story as I was with two husbands most of my twenties and thirties, but if they didn't give me sexually what I wanted, I would react with voracious anger. They suffered at the wrath of me when I was not given the validation of sex. I did not know I had been abused so I was not aware that was my pattern. Therefore, that time in my life was sexually hard driving and lonely. I didn't know I was operating under the disguise of abuse.

My inner child remembered the gentle touching by my dad, and how conflicting it was. My adult self couldn't be touched that way. Slow sex was painful and frightening. Now I know that as an adult, I can breathe into intimacy that is slow and not be the inner child, but the adult woman exploring her new claimed body. My inner child doesn't need to be present for sex at all. I can allow her to go to sleep from a day of fun and play while I have adult fun.

McKenzie Phillips spoke at an AA convention five months before I got sober and in the start of my sexual abuse counseling. She spoke about how no one believed her that she had sex with her dad because he was the famous member of the Mamas and the Papas. They said she wanted it. She was a child doing drugs with her father and he had sex with her. He was the monster. She was not.

When my dad died ten years ago, I had intuitive impulse to get clearer about something. I had no clue what. The abuse would remain buried in my subconscious for another seven years but the unraveling is all a process. I decided to get off the Effexor I had been on for 10 years for low-grade depression and panic attacks I didn't feel I had anymore. I wanted to feel all the aspects of my dad's death and not be numbed by a pill. Off Effexor I was more awake but I was also raw. Without therapy or God, I didn't know what I wanted to feel about his death. There was a nagging vague knowing I was supposed to get clear on something but I didn't know what. I had no idea it was a panic that the perpetrator was dead and with him my secret. My inner self fought to not let the dark secret die with him. Yet I couldn't claw my way to the truth. I think all my baby steps groping in the dark for clarity, and one should never look back with regret like "I should've known then and dealt with it and maybe I would still be married, or not have become such a drinker, or not been rough on my kids because I had no love in my heart yet." We can't blame ourselves for when we finally face abuse, 45, 50, 60. Yet I can't stress enough the value of therapy, support and community if you even feel there is a possibility you were abused. Our path is exactly what it is supposed to be. Even the coping skills I developed throughout a lifetime of denial have become assets today of courage, strength and empowerment. When we are talking about chasing bigger dreams post abuse discovery, no time has been wasted to get there.

Intuition is a new gift of stepping away from being ruled by your inner child. It takes the place of that young angry repressed voice as one that wants you to be on a safe, prosperous spiritual path. You start to learn the ease and grace of your intuition, and what is led by impatience, fear and destructiveness. It's not to be taken lightly "trusting your intuition." Especially when it comes to what I have coined "Shinny Object Theory." People like quick solutions to their problems, or instant fun. Small children like shinny objects. I don't need to go towards shinny objects for solutions. I have discernment and intuition.

WRITING PROMPT:

Describe what you intuition looks like versus your will. How would you describe it today? Write a scenario where you followed your intuition and the outcome was life affirming.

I don't beat myself up for any decisions or action that come from doubting my intuition but I surely listen to the voices that tells me when I am attracted to someone as "a shinny object." Any interaction on that non-intimate and unauthentic level bites me in the ass (or costs me money.) I didn't properly vet them. They seemed to be my people, like a business partner, but they were crazy all around and I was blind to it. Finding your intuition is a process of learning how to share, and even overshare, with people. You may hold back and not trust. It's an education of intuition. Lean into it. You will be the light who leads the path for others when you do that sharpening of self.

After a couple years of facing the wreckage of abuse, getting sober, recovering from Achalasia, falling in and out of love, and then surrendering finally to the fact that I don't know at all who I am ... my inner child suddenly trusted the adult me.

She no longer wanted to be trouble. I always thought I was bad adult Kim. Why couldn't I just stop making so much trouble? My first husband's father used to always tell me I was trouble. My second's husband's father said I would be alright if only I could see how fantastic I am. They didn't know they were not seeing a woman, but a trapped and mourning little girl who was in trouble. She had been real bad with her dad. She was ready for me to be able to help her, and help me, and be whole as an adult who had ambitions and an authentic voice in this world. An adult with laughter, wonder, curiosity. I could help others if I became my inner child's representative.

I started to make safe decisions for both of us, and let the little me sit back and be a kid. She could keep me in curiosity and wonder when appropriate. When to play and be light with others who were in the darkness.

WRITING PROMPT:

What would it feel like to completely play as a child? Where would you go and what would you do if no one was watching or judging? Write a child-like scene and put yourself in it as an adult.

I call for the Inner Child Movement! She/He is relevant to how authentically we live our lives. You don't have to come from a traumatized childhood to connect with your inner child. We all need the connection to understand our purest selves.

I used to think all my big, loud messy emotions were me losing my mind but now I have accepted that voice was a little girl who was never heard. Knowing this, I can temper the energy and dance with it. Connecting to our inner child will make us better lovers, friends, parents, writers, entrepreneurs and workers. We can start to be comfortable in our adult skin.

For a while in abuse recovery, my inner child wanted to make sure I knew she was deeply wounded and not to forget that. It was my job to soothe her and assure her I would never let her down, I would not forget what was done, but at some point I needed to teach that inner child it is time to live and to play without regret.

For me to have fun as an adult, not under the watchful eyes of a scared inner child, was true victory.

CHAPTER ELEVEN
SURVIVOR POWER

We build power as survivors in little steps. For the burden of recovering from abuse, you are granted an extraordinary gift to, for lack of better words, take the world by the balls. That does not mean we take the world by storm in one night. We gain inner power when we are ready. Ask yourself this: just because you came to terms with the abuse, have you given yourself permission to take your life to a new level of power and courage that is only accessible for survivors? Now is not the time to hold yourself back from a deeper life just because you "Dealt with it" and it is off your plate. It's time to rock and roll your life on a less fearful level. For me, because my denial was so huge and great, buried deep in my subconscious to the point where the concept of the abuse simply didn't exist for me until it could no longer be hidden, I had to wait until I was in my forties to come to terms with it for the first time in my life.

But that was exactly God's plan. I have a deeper appreciation of my life of rich experiences and gifts like my children, my writing and my sobriety today as a thriving abuse survivor. I loathed myself for so long that it is profound when I get to be a student of self-love. I can taste the value of it with deep gratitude. Believe me, with two little kids and a new business to stress about, I didn't want to get up every morning at 5AM and write, and lots of times I didn't. What always called me back was my message. My growth. It whispered a longing to document the gradual peeling back of the old identity for the new one and love myself in the unknown transition, no matter what took shape.

WRITING PROMPT:
Do you see new life experiences unfolding around you? Are you suppressing any levels of love for those people or experiences? Why? What scares you?

Healing takes time but at a certain point the magic of successes in your life start to come into the equation, and that is a new "problem" to cope with. Getting the life we have always wanted but never could access it from deep in our heart is actually hard! Especially while concurrently attempting to learn to love. If you came to terms with abuse when you are in your twenties, and are now in your forties reading this book, you may have had a life free of pain because you dealt with the abuse at an early age. Or you swept it under the carpet and remained disconnected. Some people were just done with the acceptance of what happened to them several decades ago and moved on. My friend who was there for me to call after I wrote my mom the email about the abuse was one of those women. Her clarity allowed her to champion women like me who can now champion other women who have repressed their pain and shameful secrets up into their forties and fifties.

About three years into the acceptance of the abuse, little identity shifts started to happen. I was not aware that these shifts in perspective were going to lead me to another even grander shift in perspective in the coming year.

Part of empowerment as an abuse survivor is the relationship with nature. I had always experienced a melancholy sadness to fall weather. It brought up loneliness, separation and a disconnection with my body. Rain in particular made me feel messy and scattered. I was not able to embrace the beauty of seasons and change. To be fully present on our earth, connecting with the seasons, and the moon, says that you are willing to explore that relationship with your spirit that was once trapped by abuse memoires. Now rainstorms excite me and I can embrace weather variation. Instead of inclement weather being trouble, it is celebratory. I look at rain as a unique gift. I never wanted unpredictability. I needed control. To know how everything was going to happen. I had been so powerless as a child to someone else's whims that I was not going to accept even God's whim with nature. I would hate and loathe it. While fall dusk can still trigger in me some kind of fear (the words that whisper in my head, "I don't want to go home"), I can look into that fear and ask God to help me someday embrace the colors of magic hour that I love as a visual person. The brightness of the day at 7 PM in the most recent time change brought me hope of a new dawning of a perception of weather. I am a witness as a newly shaped self to a variety of reactions and feelings to nature, not just dread that there was some kind of climate change that affected me adversely. I am feeling like I am a part of this earth again as a whole human for the first time.

WRITING PROMPT:

How do seasons affect you? What season creates joy and what causes feelings of loss or fear?

As a child I escaped into nature. There were six foot tall grasses in the fields surrounding my house that I could hide in. I would ride my bike down to the ocean and just hang out. I spent a lot of time with my aunt's golden retriever. She was a dear friend. I recall burying my face in her golden fur, voiceless, looking for answers to a simple "Why?" She didn't know but she provided an innocent safety. I sat in a lot of quiet as a child. I couldn't tell you what I was thinking as I have no memories of childhood thought like other people do, but I can only imagine I was wanting to escape in the most painful way.

I took two beautiful trips early on in my healing from sexual abuse and both were to be more connected with nature. I drove up to Eslan and volunteered in the gardens. I hacked at fennel until my back ached, and pulled weeds from lettuces with burning thighs.

The seals on a nearby rock barked incessantly all day. For my service, I was given access to the salt baths where men and women congregate naked. At first shy, once I laid in the bubbling warm baths with other naked strangers, and naked families, I saw freedom from shame. At night I stayed in the New Camaldoli Monastery in my own little hermitage up on the highest point in this Big Sur area, and woke in the morning to literally be over the clouds that covered the Pacific ocean. My second trip that summer was to Idylwild, a gorgeous mountain town about an hour outside Los Angeles, and stayed in a little cabin with a hammock. I laid on the hammock most of the day when I wasn't procuring food from the local supermarket or hiking in the vast silence. I read an entire book. I was with myself in nature in the most profound way.

WRITING PROMPT:

What were some of your experiences in nature as a child? How much time did you spend unsupervised from your parents? Can you be in nature now alone as an adult and what does that feel like?

After these experiences, I started to ask myself the question, what do I really want for myself on this earth? I hadn't ever really wondered beyond what I thought I was supposed to want. A marriage, children and Oscar.

Then one day it hit me like an arrow hitting a brass bowl sitting on your head. It pings and sings and resonates all around you. What are my Values?

Now I was asking myself to look right in the face what on this earth as a grown woman was I willing to stand by no matter what, and attract to my life.

I made a list of My Values:

Spirituality & God and Following my life purpose

Financial Independence and security

My Children

Sobriety/emotional sobriety

Creativity

Education
Self-worth/personal growth
Communication
A soul mate
Reliability/Honesty
Community
Nature/Ocean/Beauty
Home/Aesthetics

WRITING PROMPT:

Have you made a list of your values? Without editing or telling your-self what should be on the list, write one that really resonates with who you are today. No matter where you are in your recovery from sexual abuse, this list will continue to refine itself if you rewrite it every six months.

I was shocked how easy the list creation had been but also that woah, God and spirituality are my top values? Not a man? Not being sexy or rich? In fact a significant romantic relationship was not even close to the top of my list. I wanted to change it and erase it and say, "Well that's not right. I am a total romantic that loves to be with men and have been reading relationship and love books to hone in on my soul mate." But the truth is I want to be living my life in my true values as a newly healed woman before I can attract a partner who could bring his same high level of value and standards that I set for myself.

To support and uphold these values, I signed up with a life coach. Something I had never ever endeavored to do. I thought it was a frivolous waste of time working on myself. I had profound experiences working with Clare. She is one of the best. Strong and willing to hold space. She taught me it's the saboteur voice in my head that says things like, "Who do you think you are to dream like that? " or "Trite little fool, hapless dreamer." She taught me how to talk to that saboteur or in other words, "Tell the little fucker to take a hike." She taught me how to step out beyond survival and say to the universe "I'm going to blossom." She taught me how to have survivor power. The "wow" aspect. When I quieted the self-defeating voices, I was blown away by so many aspects of life like the light in the trees, a writing class, the laughter of my children, the ocean, reading a great book or sitting at my desk and wondering what I would write about now. I was given a new beginning and it was wonderful.

Then she asked me, "What is it going to take for you to just be okay with everything you are doing?" I didn't know the answer then but I know now...Love for self unconditionally, and time. I didn't want to waste any more time getting better but over time I simply did get better under good direction. I didn't need to strive for perfection by any means. When I am perfect I am actually dead. I understood that I had been beating myself up my whole life. I was exhausted.

WRITING PROMPT:

Have you been beating yourself up? If so it's time to put down the whip and start to thrive in your life. Identify in a list all the areas in which you beat yourself and the voices that talk to you about it.

As I understood I had power over my mind and body through positive talk and self love, the long lasting full blown chest ripping anxiety attacks minimized to once every couple months. I wish I could say they are completely gone, but I have the awareness now of their arrival. Little warning twinges of anxiety in my esophagus would be followed by an ever so slight chest constriction. If knowing these warning signs, I still escalate to a full-blown attack, it is no one's fault but my own. I was obsessing in my head about something I had no time or place to be worrying about and my body reminded me it was old negative behavior. I also saw the attacks were residual repressed gook still melting away. I had left the present, God, hope and fell out of trust all would be as it should. The question that life coach Clare asked which correlates to having attacks is, "Am I okay with who I am today?" Some days that question is not so easily answered because I am continually changing as I heal from the abuse. Yet, if I intellectualize that concept, I will remove myself from the present and God, and I will allow room and space for anxiety. I need to be always okay with who I am now. Period.

Another powerful change is to not dread being alone. I used to or think there was something wrong with me if I was home alone on a Saturday night. I have many modes of fun at my fingertips, and if girlfriends are not available to go to the movies or a concert, I can go by myself. I look to be around people in this beautiful world with so many fascinating activities, sounds and colors, but I can also be with me. I did not get sober and face abuse to sit alone on the couch every weekend like I was still smoking pot and using alcohol or in my unhappy marriage. I am alone and appreciating all the little parts of life like a bath, a book, a call with a friend, a good show. I slowly, in its own time, let my new life and my connection with my Higher Power help me make a course correction. I also learned I don't need to fix everything that troubles me right away. There is a good chance that the negative brain is finding something wrong when there is nothing wrong. I'm used to high alert. I got good at it when I would listen for the abuse coming. I don't have to handle high alert in the same way because I am protected by my knowledge and my intuition as a fully realized adult self in survivor power.

For example, one weekend, I made a choice to not go out to a party and stay home in the rain and make myself a healthy dinner and read a new Victorian novel someone had long ago suggested. I got it from the library. My brain tried to tell me I was a spinster home alone with the cat. I gave myself permission to ignore my mind and know I am not THAT woman, but simply enjoying comfort with self. I gain strength and power when the time comes to go after my dreams from honoring my self. I have a full life that needs down time to let there be manifestation within my values. I realize that despite the negative connotation of the word "alone", I was starting to be at peace with one-ness of self. I am glad I had that glorious chance to lay on the couch with a book because life got super busy again and I didn't have another chance for months!

So don't doubt experiences! You never know when you will not have them again because your life is getting so packed!

Another subtle change in building my power as a survivor was when I agreed to believe that my current family was okay made up of just my kids and I. Originally I would try and date men who I thought would be the right candidates to complete our family but I was flying under the radar of my standards. A family needs a 4th person, right? I had also never blown up pictures of the girls and I. I had resisted by first telling myself the pictures were too expensive. Then asking, who puts pictures up on the wall of just three? Then the day came that I realized I was not doing my girls and I a service by not being confident in our family nucleus. My omission created falsity. So I blew up and picture of the three of us, and a picture I loved of the two of them a bit littler and it went over the TV. I had gone through a very tumultuous life under an untold secret- I could do anything dynamic now! Even if to others putting up that picture would be easy to do, for me it was a big victory.

WRITING PROMPT:

What can you change about your environment to reflect your new values? Do you feel proud of the family you have built?

You start to have a new relationship with time when you come into your power as a survivor. You are not filling every second to avoid facing abuse. When I started to honor time to let my life unfold instead of controlling every second of it, my life was filled with more unexpected wonders and an expansion of life experiences. Time expanded as I willed myself to look at it positively. The abuse took time away from you not just in the acts themselves, but the years of mourning. Now you don't have to rush to not think. The demons won't get you anymore. You have earned the right to start living. Our desire to show love and kindness grows, and you need time to achieve that goal. I take small spaces of time, 10 minutes here and there to build on an idea, to record an epiphany, to make a call to someone to ask a question. These pieces may seem non consequential in terms of time investment, but they are even more valuable than the hours I would force myself to "learn" something or "drive an idea to fruition." My life projects come together in an ease and flow that is unimaginable. I suddenly know how to work within time as part of happiness. Can you imagine this for you? How does that feel to believe you have all the time to create, love, feel and breathe? If you are not there yet, it is okay. These changes come slowly, but when they do, it is powerful. More powerful than for people that have not been abused. You get that 'eyes wide open benefit' to say, "Wow" because it is so radically different than the time perspective of abuse.

WRITING PROMPT:

What areas of your life are you not believing you have enough time, or where would you like to spend more time?

The magic of healing is I can shine as bright as I want on any given day. It is limitless. In my new power of my realized self, I can see small miracles of wonder and delight and enjoy my fellow people in the world. I understand life is not a race to the end. The poison is out of my body. I am no longer the angry tiger with the thorn in his paw. I am a bright white dove in the sky. I can soar and be a full human. I am not halved or punctured anymore. Yet the scars I carry of the battle remind me to be so much more every day than my little mind believes. The miracles play all around me. I don't want to miss a single one of them.

CHAPTER TWELVE
BLAME LIES BETWEEN
FEAR AND SHAME

I looked it up the origin of the word 'shame'? It had Germanic origins. The Greeks had a positive definition of shame as "modesty". I have never heard of or experienced shame in any way that was positive. For me, all shame is downright hideous. Even if it is indicating I have done an action that could require apology or correction, I don't want to be ashamed about it. I can be enlightened and remorseful, but even remorse is the gateway for shame. To get away from shame, I pointed the finger at others. You did this to me, you did that to me. I berated lovely people, and I walked away from friendships. I was a victim. Shame was the gateway emotion to all the addictive and destructive coping behaviors that kept me surviving my life in denial from sexual abuse.

In recovery, I would not allow shame to live in my mind or body anymore. I sensed my healing was entering a new frontier. A place I had never been before. I had lived my life under such a thick cloak of fear that I would be exposed for my secrets and shamed. I made sure life stayed just small enough to complain and be angry, but not be seen for the bright light that I had the capacity to be. Now I had no more secrets and I was opening my mind and my heart to all the possibilities life could throw at me. At first, everything felt super dangerous. I didn't know who or what I could trust. That intuitive sense of knowing was there, but I didn't trust it as my heart-centered truth. I started to learn that abuse survivors when they step into their healing are very deeply intuitive. Some even become psychics and empathic. I decided I had nothing to lose and moved in a direction in my life where I could have what I believed I wanted.

I was so tired of beating myself up in shame from fear-based actions. We are shamed when we are little and then we carry that shame into our adult lives and we shame others. When I wake up every day, I ask God to help me with what I fear. If I am clear of my fears, I can own them and not come into contact with the wrong people who confirm these fears. I become "bad." I don't do well when I am in the state of a bad little girl.

WRITING PROMPT:

Write about what makes you feel shame every day. Start to notice where you feel ashamed. Are you allowing others to set you off in the shame spiral? Or are you the culprit of your own shame. Then share with a trusted loving confidant.

When my emotional net widened and my life took on more dimensions, I grew accepting of behaviors of others that drove me crazy before. It was far from perfection, but I could feel appreciation not just annoyance when my ten year old sang loudly in the bathtub, or compassion when my six year old stubbornly cried when she didn't get her way. This used to be so unbearable to me (these intrusive child noises) and now they are the sounds of a full life. Other people expressing who they are and I don't have to be the one to punish them because I was silenced for so long. It's my responsibility to curb my angry outbursts when I don't like what is happening in my life, my house, when I am grossly overtired. These angry outbursts would lead to day-killing shame later. They are just not worth it.

WRITING PROMPT:

Without shame about it, write about a knee-jerk reaction you had that was based in fear. Really enjoy examining the way you behaved.

We need to have a chuckle at our crazy selves sometimes to give us permission to get better.

I was always a runner to elude the repercussions of blame. I ran from my dad and mom as a little girl when they would chase me because I had mouthed off. I recall them cornering me under the bed or my dad chasing me around a kitchen table. I was scared. I was not an actual runner as a kid (I hated cross country) but I became a long distance runner when my second marriage was failing. All through that marriage, I ran from the moments I didn't like with a powerful conviction and rage. I would storm off from very volatile arguments into the streets of London, San Francisco, Berkeley and Los Angeles. Often with no money, drunk and in high heels. Sound familiar? You don't love me so you don't get love, mother fucker. You are wasting my life away. That high state of anxiety for so many years was what finally bottomed me out. My addictions were just seepage from the portals in me that were sliced open from such lack of self-care and continual shame. An IV of shame. I smacked into brick walls all the time running, looking over my shoulder to see if shame was going to catch me.

Since I have gotten healed from the abuse, and in recovery from addictions, the compulsion to run in such an enraged manner subsided. I don't get to the boiling point from the fear as often. I don't want to run unless it's for actual exercise and even then, if I had my preference I would wander on a long walk. I may complain and feel incredibly doubtful and uncomfortable, but I don't run. I sit in the space and listen to myself start to spin into negativity and I think, "Is this where I want to be?" The answer is almost always "No."

When I was a child, I had to run from my mother's rigidity, especially after the divorce of my parents. She had no emotional bandwidth for me. She screamed, I hated her, and I moved out at thirteen into the home of my abuser.

I recall having a car ride with my mother in 1995. I was twenty-five and directing a small film I had put my heart and soul into. She was driving to the movie set with me somewhere in NJ and I completely lost all sense of direction on the highway. This was before cell phones, and GPS so if you didn't know where you were going, and you didn't have a map, you'd better ask. We got terribly lost and I flipped out. I raged at my mother so hard in the car. Decades of bottled up blame and unsaid words. I was a lunatic. I felt a combination of sadistic horror and glee by what I put her through in that car. I was 25 and nothing in my childhood had been healed. No one had talked about anything. She took in the velocity of it on that day and we didn't speak of it again, or find the why behind it. Hence my abuse stayed hidden.

I would continue to rage at and blame anyone who became a fixture in my life until I walked into Alanon almost fifteen years later on my knees to God and saw I was yelling just to have my young soul finally witnessed and heard.

My ten year old became a runner like me, as early in her childhood I did not have the capacity to give her feelings and emotions space. She was in my way at night when I wanted to get buzzed or stoned on the couch and she wouldn't go to bed. As she got older, and I got healthier, she realized she could run away from any conflict with rage. She had the power to hit me. She could start to revolt against all that repression. She blamed me for how she felt.

As I healed and continued to emotionally show up for her, I was granted a miracle. She stopped running. It happened over helping her with math. My dad had a short temper helping me with math, and so I never asked and would fail tests. So I made a pact I would stick in there with my kids' schoolwork, especially math! Typically in the past, the way my math help with her would go is we would start with me calmly explaining the work, and in seconds she would go off the rails, yelling and shaking in the corner that she would never understand the work. I felt incredibly helpless. Then she would tell me to leave her alone and I would think, she can't do this alone. She doesn't need to do this alone. But I was powerless. All I could do was love her as she was.

This time was different. We were sitting down to do fractions and as I started to explain, typical to the pattern above, within five seconds she was escalating into "I don't understand" mode. Then I saw her flinch. Her whole body wanted to run…but she stayed.

"Wow, you stayed. You stuck it," I acknowledged.

The look on her face said she knew exactly what I meant. She didn't want to run from a conversation with me, or her difficulties. She wanted my help, and she in that moment with staying told me she trusted me. That I wouldn't be volatile, mean and run from her either. She had witnessed my healthy new behavior over some time, and she was willing to bank on the fact that there didn't need to be pain and escape anymore, but rather love and understanding. It was a freeing moment for both of us. I was able to help her at ten. No one was able to help me at ten but I could reverse the pattern of the family history. This was a parallel universe two women of different generations were walking through. I was convinced she would always be a runner. I had prayed to God about it. This can happen for you too when you unwrap your abuse and recover. Generations can be saved by stopping the psychological patterns of abuse.

WRITING PROMPT:

Where have you seen your family change their behavior as you grew less volatile and ashamed?

I have had to work through a lot of shame and regret about all the people I treated poorly, including myself, because I was hiding deep in the shame of the abuse. My kids went to therapy to cope with the divorce but they truly healed when I faced the sexual abuse, alcoholism and put my shame away. Now, several years later as I write this book, and I have healed and am a radically different present loving mom my children trust immensely. My shame became self-love. Don't doubt it. It can happen. The dark corners of shame can fade into bright open hope.

WRITING PROMPT:

Do you still blame yourself for actions done to others when you were in the throes of sexual abuse denial? What would it feel like to let that lift off of you?

At some point it's non-negotiable that you put shame away forever. Gone. Obliterated. Don't even make excuses as an adult for it to come back. There are other emotions you can feel for actions such as sadness or anxiety usually linked to a fear of being judged, or regret for a behavior that you can amend. As our actions stabilize, we have less to regret or apologize for. Old shame makes us blame people in our current world. Suspicious thinking about their motives because they may be out to get us. Sure, have a healthy protective gage with others, but know that typically someone who has proven trustworthy to you is not out to get you. They are not igniting your shame so you can blame them for an action they did which was minor in comparison to your accusation. My mind can still accuse people I love because of my expectations and judgment of how I should be treated.

I apologize to the men reading this book, but I would be irresponsible if I didn't mention Premenstrual Syndrome. It heightens and exacerbates all my feelings of shame, blame and fear. I have been convinced my boyfriend is telling me devious lies, that I will be bankrupt, schedules with work and the kids suddenly feel overwhelming…I could go on, but what is profound, is now that I am sober, and have taken my body back from the secrets of abuse, I can walk through PMS with awareness. I keep a period tracker on my phone that tells me when PMS starts, and I take PMS herbs right at the ten-day mark. I don't make any major decisions during the ten days of PMS because my underlying emotions at this time are fear, shame and blame. I advise you to look at your menstrual calendar and tune in to your body so you understand certain reactions at these times of the month.

As my life grew more consciously precious, I no longer could squander days on this earth in shame. When I stopped shaming myself for not doing enough, I started celebrate me. You would think that would be a relief. It was one of the hardest concepts for me to swallow. The old me did not celebrate. The old me ran from any emotions that required me to trust and surrender. It was a hard way to live life. I carried a thick hard shell around on my body until I trusted the identification of these negative experiences I once considered a part of my life every day. I don't need to think like this. I was able to make a decision to stop the spiraling pattern of despair and ask people that are in more confidence and joy to show me a better life.

I had to learn when I got sober to pat myself on the back and say, "Good job. That's enough for today." For someone who is dying to be seen, heard and understood, I was not comfortable with the spotlight on me in any way, yet at the same time I was dying for attention.

WRITING PROMPT:

What is your most shameful secret? Write it out first and then tell it to someone you trust. Then set it free.

For my forty-sixth birthday, I had one of the parties of my dreams. No, there was not a band, and unlimited shrimp cocktail. It was in my small and comfy apartment. I had close to twenty women pot luck style come over and trim my artificial Christmas tree with the ornaments that had been collected all through my childhood, some adulthood and my children's childhoods. The experience was warm, safe, and to be honest, as people ate and sang karaoke, and put ornaments on the tree, it was not just all for me. I had provided a place for many different women of different backgrounds and personalities to come together and commune on a Sunday afternoon. I thanked my kids when I blew out the candles. They had tirelessly helped me throw the party. Something shifted for them that day too. They saw a full mom. A happy woman who was finally wholehearted and clear when she said, "I want to play."

WRITING PROMPT:

Where in your life, and with who particularly, are you most comfortable sharing new parts of you? Where do you still hold back celebrating and why?

I thought nailing this "celebration concept" could take a long time, especially if I had to keep creating the celebrations. It was so foreign to me. It was always risky. I'm tired. I don't have time to create reasons to celebrate. They talk about waiting for the other shoe to drop. For me it was the big fat meaty hand of the Universe squashing me right in the midst of a happy squeal. I felt that because of the shame of the past, of not accomplishing enough, of partying too hard, of cheating on men, of lack of compassion for my children, I'd never get a second chance.

I felt like the wall would tumble down if I showed too much cocky joy to "the life camera". These reactions are entangled with lack of trust, and a hesitance to surrender. The solution is befriending the middle ground, not only seeing the highs and lows of experiences. Calm, thoughtful and intuitive is not something I ever thought I would be. Yet the celebrations come in the most profound and gratifying way with simple planning and foresight with my intuition.

The progress is I know that the celebrations ARE coming and they take me far away from shame. The Universe is gifting me exactly what I need and deserve, and I don't have to feel shame if I say, "That was real win, Universe. Thank you." While it still can be challenging for me to celebrate – which by the way could be simply time relaxing on the beach on a Sunday for a week well done-the process of celebration has taken a deeper dimension in my life. When we celebrate, there is no room for shame.

When I was a substitute teacher during my recovery, I had a class where a boy was always knocking all his colored pencils all over the floor. It was very distracting to his work.

"Why don't you get a pencil case?" I asked him.

He shrugged. "My mom won't buy me one."

What could I say to that? In Culver City, shocking poverty exists in the homes of some of these kids.

That night I recalled mugs on my porch someone moving had given me as planters. They had cities on them. I took the Tokyo one and figured it could hold pencils. I brought it in the next day and plopped it on his desk.

"For your pencils," I said, "And I don't want to see you distracted from your work with them again." I felt pretty good about my kindness and he was clearly pleased with the gift. I showed love to a stranger. I could've doubted whether I was enough to show up like that with a mug but I didn't. I operated from the heart without shame.

Here's the best part of the story. A whole year later, no longer a sub teacher, I pick my daughter up from school and I see the kid. He points at me and says, "You were the teacher who gave me the Tokyo mug for my pencils."

I nodded.

He smiled. "I still have it."

That was a win of wins. Satisfaction and warmth spread over my whole body. A grin involuntarily took to my face. I allowed myself to feel good. I celebrated but I didn't use it to be more than it was. I knew I wanted to do kind things like that again. Then I moved on.

I can celebrate all kinds of constant joys with gratitude and I can celebrate opportunity passing or landing because it is all in the flow and flux of life. Everything is passed to me from God's hand.

WRITING PROMPT:

What have been some of your wins lately that can be celebrations? Little acts of faith, or unexpected gifts given or received, tangible or verbal? Write about how it felt even if you feel shame for honoring yourself.

We can set ourselves free from shame and fear, and therefore blaming others through understanding our core self, our values, and accepting our life day by day in its celebrations and wins. We can also build trust with others by confessing our moments of shame. Sharing the secrets takes the power out of them, and through the eyes of others, we can see that we weren't so bad after all.

CHAPTER THIRTEEN
STUFF HOLDS MEMORIES

Abuse survivors can hold themselves hostage to reoccurring trauma from the past. They may not even notice because the triggers are very covert, and they still believe they don't have the worth to live in better circumstances. We react, and then label ourselves "overreactive" and pray these uncomfortable nagging signs go away. In recovery, these unnecessary holds to the past return until addressed. We now operate with a deeper awareness of self-love and confidence so the insistent feelings can't be ignored, and we make new choices.

One of my holds in the past manifested in the couch I still had after twelve years. For some, having a couch that long is not an issue, but for me, it was coming home day in and day out and sitting on the same couch that retained the energy of twelve years drinking and smoking pot, fucking with an unconscious disconnected heart, and fighting and brooding with a simmering rage and anger. Sure there were sweet memories…the couch was an unusually big couch. My oldest daughter when she was two would get behind these big cushions on play dates with friends and hide. It was adorable, but I was so removed from joy and so put upon in my life by a heaviness I had not identified in my heart, I knew even those memories were half seen by me. I had wanted the couch originally because it was really big and gave lots of space. I was real into making sure that there was enough space for me to disappear and to hide. I see now how much I wanted to always have barriers from people, when in fact I had the biggest barriers inside myself.

I had kept the couch living divorced in my own apartment this long with all its stagnating memories for the reason of practicality but the truth is, the minute I knew something was very wrong about still owning that couch, I should have acted on it. Instead, I loathed the couch for another three years. I was working as a substitute teacher making crap money and couldn't possibly think about entertaining the cost of a new couch, yet I had thousands of dollars in my savings account. As I started to grow in confidence as a business owner, and healing as a survivor, I had a shift in thinking about money and abundance. I still didn't know when my next client would sign or how the bills every month would get paid, but I did know that every time I came in my apartment and saw that couch, I would feel ugly, dirty and shameful. It was no longer aligning with my new positive thought pattern. I remained plunged into the past and all the expectations I put on myself on that couch. Also it was dirty from use, and I had given up dry cleaning it, and my new mantra with my kids was to take all their school clothes off before they came near the couch. "Don't dirty the couch," became my afterschool mantra. This is funny because spiritually that couch was filthier than they would ever make it. I knew I had to let it go.

I expressed this feeling to a money intuit book client in one of our sessions. She was amazing at what she did, and I needed someone to confess my coach woe to.

"I hate the couch," I confessed to her. "Whenever I walk in the door I see it and it makes me feel poor and sad and saggy. When my kids are at their dads, I don't even want to sit on the couch and watch a movie. I mean, I do want to be alone and watch the movie, just not on that couch."

"Get rid of it immediately, " she said. "Give it to people who will love the couch as much as you hate it. And send me a text when it's gone".

Telling her this truth allowed me to let go of the couch that reminded me of my past sicker self. We can be prisoners to our secrets and this was a big shameful one. A thrilled couple got the couch the day I put it on Craig's list and I even threw in the coffee table as well. They had no furniture and were building a life. They would have no baggage with my couch. They could be free to do whatever was in their destiny on that couch. I hope the couch brought them the hope that it gave me when I let it go.

WRITING PROMPT:

What can you get rid of today that you are holding on to as clutter or bad energy?

I gave away with that couch all the men I slept with, incidents very fueled by a mind numbed by alcohol or weed and the desperate need to be loved. I gave away all the fights with my ex husband about not enough sex and all the times he or I slept on the couch because we hated each other and had no idea how to pull ourselves out of the dark hole. I also am a very intense orgasmer who gushes. So I would make a mess of the couch and have to clean it like a bad dog. I felt like that. A bad dog. I was so desperate for you to have sex with me and validate what my worth is, an object to be penetrated, I would forgo the couch and just make a mess of it. Then cushions would have to be placed everywhere to dry. It was exhausting and mind filling and not even worth it. But I would be satisfied too. Look what I did. Good dog. Wag your tail. Good dog. I can't believe I am writing this right now but we have to be honest and open about our bodies as abuse survivors. I have the words. My reaction to being pleasured is not a dirty thing. It is another gift from God.

My brain's dark thoughts when the couch was leaving were, "You are impetuous and crazy." Isn't that funny? Over the freedom to get a new couch? (A year later that same voice returned when I booked tickets to take my daughters to Spain but I had built up a muscle of resistance to it. I had learned from that couch, and we happily went to Spain.)

The couch leaving also brought up my lack of commitment to any values, dreams and desires in recovery. One foot in and one foot out was my operating system yet I explained it to anyone who would listen as "exploring my options." That doesn't produce million dollars results or life long marriages, especially when those options are not found in a bottle of alcohol or an obsessive spiritually decrepit panic. Now I would have to instate a level of surrender to a 100% commitment, no wavering, and slow down long enough to have a discussion with my God. Eventually it would also extend to partners and advisors, but now it was practice time with God, and an unknown couch. Joining AA had been my first real commitment for life besides parenting. Committing to recover from sexual abuse no matter what was the second life commitment. Now I had those foundations to apply in expanding my life.

WRITING PROMPT:

What are you 100% committed to in your life? Write about how it makes you feel to be committed no matter how minor a choice.

There I sat in the space in the apartment without a couch. A new hole I created to be filled. What kind of couch would the new me buy? The abundance of possibilities morphed into panic. What do I love? I was stuck in my limited experiences. I knew buying big stuff in the past felt forced and unaligned. I understood God was with me in every area of my life, and I would need to wait for divine guidance on the couch. What scared me most about buying my first adult piece of furniture alone and sober was the message to the Universe that I was ready to build the home of the life of the real me – not the false me that lived under the lies and devastation of the abuse. I deserved to surround myself with beauty in my apartment no matter how uncomfortable that made me feel.

The kids and I continued to "camp" in the living room, and I prayed for what I wanted to reveal itself in the most natural way. The vision you have of your whole life is reflected by your surroundings, and so I was taking this first step seriously.

Then one day I knew. I wanted a blue velvet couch. Gaudy? Tacky? Hell no! Awesome!

My friend Jeff made me the couch. Of course, this whole time of couch vision questing, he was right under my nose. A year prior

I had stapled swatches in his warehouse for $10 an hour to pay for Christmas presents for the kids. Now he was making me a couch. It was incredible. Instead of panicking as I wrote the check for the couch, I had confidence in my new-found maturity that money comes and goes, and the money spent for this couch would be replenished. Then I sat on my new blue couch and surveyed the rest of the apartment.

Everything else was so fucking brown!

How on earth did I accumulate so much mahogany furniture? Nothing had color. I had been living externally what I had felt inside. Like shit.

Now I was becoming a woman who wanted more color and vibrancy in her life. I was willing to go find it. Then I had to quell the desire to change everything right then and there. The journey is the fun, not the destination. One needs to have the awareness, then the acceptance, then take the action, which is often easy when it is God guided! I etched in my mind a road map to de-mahogany my place.

Clearing the couch was the catalyst for my new direction of thinking. The couch was a profound metaphor for all areas of my life. I had to slowly allow in what was fitting for the new me. I hoped for a partner to create memories with on my new couch. There still will spills and arguments, but there will be a deeper understanding on this couch. It won't be the couch of conflict but rather the couch of connection.

The next step was looking at what I wore and put in my office, and on my walls and interior decorating my new life. Look at me, Life!

WRITING PROMPT:

Look around your surroundings and honestly ask yourself what doesn't make you happy. What holds you back from expressing aesthetics that you may prefer? Write about what it feels like to embrace new desires or likes. Is it liberating or confusing? Write about both spectrums.

Chapter Fourteen
Making Adult Commitments

G rowing up, I was forced into commitments I didn't choose. Sexual abuse the glaring one, but also playing the piano, and attending an all girls' school where I was bullied and unhappy. I was forced to stick to circumstances I didn't want, and I was also taught, when people are done with you, they cut you off. I would grow up to make commitments haphazardly, in desperation and fear, and then find myself in misery years later, awkwardly cutting out and running. It was not until sexual abuse recovery and sobriety that I had to take a long hard look at my commitment evasion. I joined a business group of women and the lifetime membership was $450, on top of which I paid $50 every month to attend the lunch. I was not getting any leads and I was pissy about it. I would leave in a negative huff. Another luncheon spent with women who didn't seem to understand my business, and industrialized chicken. I called my AA sponsor.

"These women are clearly not my people," I said, a bitter victim. "And now I have paid all this money for a lifetime membership."

My inner critic wanted me feel like an outsider, confused and hapless to levels of success.

"Can you give it a year?" she asked. "Then you can leave."

I knew she was right before I answered. Here was an opportunity to practice patience in a commitment. I was treating the group like a romantic relationship. I go in all pie in the sky expecting you to give me my dreams, but the first indication that you are not part of my illusion, I am ready to bolt out the door, write you off, and resent you for not giving me what I want and need.

I learned in AA to look at the similarities not the differences, AND to be of service. How could I use that philosophy with the women at the networking meeting? How could I change my expectations of commitment as a businesswoman? Could I help someone I met? I could think about their businesses so my ears would be open for referrals for them, instead of what I could get. When you come from abuse, you have not received a core consideration. You were taken from, so you can become a taker. As survivors, we can feel we deserve retribution from everyone and everything and get real nasty if we don't get it. That is not our fault. The abuse wired us that way, and it surely isn't the fault of people who come in our path. With help, we can be logical about who we want to align with, and make choices. Yet when we commit from the heart, we want to follow through. It is a practice in humility in abuse recovery to turn the tide and give to others on your own terms, and for your new set of values.

Therefore making commitments was to be a new slow learning process, in order to eliminate old abuse reactivity and fear. As I asked the women at the networking group more questions about their businesses, I met my stylist, financial advisor, hair dresser and branding coach. They were people I could trust with the new me because I had taken all those months to get to know them. Building of trust with others was not something I had ever committed to in the long haul. My commitment to this membership didn't take away who I was. Instead it expanded my support tribe. Eventually I was elected an officer of the group, given a member of the month award, and in time, moved on because I had changed my business model for networking. It was not done in a huff, or a tizzy, but rather organically with courtesy. Who is this woman? I was quite pleased with myself.

WRITING PROMPT:

What commitment do you currently have that irks you? Write about why this commitment bothers you and see how you could give more. What is your resistance?

The final frontier was a commitment to reduce the emotional pain in missing my kids when they went to their dads. When I started to gain self-acceptance, and stopped hiding my feelings behind dead end relationships with men, the pain of my kids leaving my home became brutal because I had finally accessed a deep love for them. My heart was thawing out. I hurt so much when they went away for a new reason. Loneliness had been replaced by genuine love. I had to fully sit in the fact that I was allowing myself to learn how to love in a completely new way. I also had to be willing to grow my new life when they were not around. I couldn't stop growing to show them their mom is more than okay. She is committed to a new self.

I decided to stop punishing myself for the marriage I wrecked or my abusive past that somehow caused me to not be with my children 100% of the time. Clearly because of what I have walked through in life, I have a greater purpose, and these arrangements free up time for me to follow that story and share it like I am here in this book. It is a bitter pill to swallow when I want to hold them and nurture them on a night I don't have them, but often that is because of my insecurity. They will be loved by me when they come home, and they are loved by their dad. Besides, who knows what journey my children will have one day from living in two homes with two happy parents. It may affect them more positively than living with two miserable checked out enraged parents who hate being married to each other.

The failed "image of family and marriage" is a grieving process. If you are reading this and have children you share in custody or have lost your children perhaps to a past of pain that you could not rise above until now, then commit to continue to be the woman you want to be. Continue to learn what you love. It will all sort out exactly as it should. Shutting down serves no one and it is a waste to the vessel of your body that contains your spirit that has a divine purpose on this earth. That is not to be taken lightly. You are in a commitment in your existence on this earth, and you can change that course no matter what was done to you.

In the weekends that I am apart from my kids now, I enjoy physical, social and romantic activities. I commit to fun, personal development and self-care. I can't fritter my life away on drinking or unavailable men, or the anxiety hole. I tap into the woman I am becoming and when my kids are in my home, I can present myself as a strong brave role model. They feel it.

Just the other day, my eleven year pitched my book coaching services to her new dentist. I had met her at one of my networking circles, and impressed, brought my daughter there for better support through the braces process. After the appointment, the dentist gave me discount cards to share with friends.

"I will definitely give these out for you," I said. "Happy to help."

"Thank you," said the Dentist.

"And you can make sure to refer clients to my mom," chimed in my daughter. "She's a great book coach!"

Man, was I proud she wanted to help promote me!

If you are a parent, then you understand the moments where you don't want to get another glass of bedtime milk, or are tired of playing referee to fights. Sure, it can suck taking care of two other creatures on top of yourself, especially if you are continuously healing. I have found that being with them is this incredible gift that I had never seen before on such a deeper level. My commitment has deepened beyond just their care and consideration, but to my life unfolding with them in it however that looks. It is easier to love someone from a distance than to really love them, because then they won't disappoint you when they act in a certain way, or they go away and you are left alone with these deep feelings of love. My new story is I am a successful woman who chooses to spend the day with her children, not she has to. I also don't waste the time when I am with them worrying about my next dollar, or lost in the fantasy of some man who isn't part of the current equation,

WRITING PROMPT:

Write a new story that puts you in a commitment worry-free. It can be with your children, an aging parent, a lover, a co-worker ... If you don't have any commitments, write about your stand on not committing.

Once we learn new values with our commitments, including patience and service, we are able to take wiggle room here and there. I was at Disney on Ice with my daughters, and taking a day off work as well as knowing I would buy them pizza later got me into a lecture mode (that was shrouded in a scarcity mentality).

"I'm not buying any crappy toys from China of spinning princesses. If you want a toy, you have your money with you. Also, I am not buying food at the venue. We are having pizza dinner after," I told them.

Okay, I sound harsh, but kids need to understand money doesn't grow on trees.

Please shoot me now for just saying that.

The moral of the story is when I had stuck to my principles in the past to save $5 on event food, or game room tickets or (insert child expectation), I had miserable kids, and fell into a silent fury at their lack of gratitude (or my burst expectations). This time, when we all got a little hungry, I bought the damn snacks. The old depravity rose up in me as I stood in line to buy $15 nachos and a pretzel but I pushed through it. We all snacked on toxic crap but were happy. The biggest victory was as we were leaving, my eight year old surveyed the toys for sale.

"You're right, mom," she said. "They are all crap from China and they're not getting MY money."

This experience was also preparing us for our trip to Spain where we would all work with a daily budget for food as a team. I did not know then, but I was preparing myself for a much bigger commitment. Or should I say, God was.

WRITING PROMPT:

What are some of your stories where you changed your limitations and what opened for you were bigger opportunities to grow in safe life-affirming way?

I have lived my life for so long on the dollars of worry and doubt and it never got me anywhere faster or brought me any more real joy. Synthetic joy perhaps, false gratification, but not this pure love I am able now to feel for my children that was blocked by the childhood where I was not held and loved and given security.

I commit to understanding every day why I think the way I do, and to believe that I have the right to have my thoughts, but I also have the tools to understand where I may be running from commitment, or putting the wrong expectations on a life that has far bigger and better plans for me. I am committed to the journey of the new me.

Chapter Fifteen
Spirituality As A Process

People who are in pain and have no outlets to heal cause other people pain. I don't have proof, but I believe my father was abused. In his repression, shame and pain, he could only do what he had been taught. Abuse. Dead ten years now, many new understandings of my dad came through simple meditation and talks with God. He helped me to shine a different light on the abuse and my abuser. Never did God ask me to forgive, but I saw a painful human journey that began way before me.

After I accepted I was an abuse survivor, I was stuffing a new life into the old container. I was painfully and acutely aware that was not a working model for my new life. I desperately needed a spiritual partner. I could not return to the God of childhood as that spirit was tainted by the abuse. I also couldn't splash around in a goblet of alcohol and call upon God. That was a falsified inebriated God. I had to create a new cup with God. A bigger God sized cup that had room for all the parts of my new life to splash around, new waterfalls of goodness to drench my cup.

Okay, enough with the cup and liquid metaphors.

I started the process to create my own God.

Call him or her your higher power, call it a sun goddess if you may, call it the ocean, but I needed to know out there was a power greater than myself who I speak to in the depths of my despair, "God help me to not feel so broken. Help me to stand tall in the face of fear. Help me to not feel so sexually frightened. Please help me to believe I will do the right thing even if it is wrong at the moment because that is part of the spiritual path." I desired the strength of a woman stretching my limitations while also being vulnerable and seeking human touch, seeking love. Where is God? In the gentle adoration of a child's freckled nose? In sexuality without shame? In jazz music playing in the background? God is solutions and non-endings, and a steady even middle. God is self-love. My new God emerged with me at the pace I could handle the path to love. It was not mechanical or forced. The spiritually gradually was in everything I embraced. My higher power had grown to be slowly over the last four years someone I could trust would be there for me to land when I risked turning off the "monkey mind" that had kept me alert to danger.

In spirituality, I found it wild as a survivor to realize that we must actually come to terms with surrender. When I read Michael Singer's The Surrender Experiment, I was blown away by the levels of surrender he went with when calls to action that were not his game plan fell before him. He had results beyond his limited human capacity. God helped me set the pace to what I could handle and when in terms of recovery from sexual abuse. God would give me a lot, or a little, and sometimes, a little was the perfect a lot.

WRITING PROMPT:

What does surrender look like for you? Where does surrender make you uncomfortable but you see the benefits when you let go?

Lying there at night as a child, silenced by the abuse taking place, and having no voice to ask the why questions, I disconnected from myself as well as God. Yet I distinctly remember praying to him alone from my bed. I knew his power because I would say "God I hate my parents, please make them die." Then later I would fear that he could actually do that, and I would say, "God, I take that back. I love my parents and they don't deserve to die." I feared my power of making my wishes come true with my God. Yet, I don't know if I ever asked him to make the abuse stop.

As the Big Book in Alcoholics Anonymous says, God was everything or nothing. Now that I had God ever present in my life 95% of the time, okay maybe 75%, I was willing to believe that God had been with me the whole time I was being abused speaking to me but as a child I could not hear. What he was saying was, someday child, while it may not seem so today, or tomorrow, this experience you have will be part of your journey to share and help heal others.

God does not make people do bad things. People do bad things. God just assures us that this too will come to pass in peace and service. I started to notice I had new strengths of character, and a sudden confidence in actions. As I grew into my new being with a spiritual partner, I could speak in front of groups without a pounding heart or affected breathing. I could start to track and understand when and why the anxiety attacks hit.

WRITING PROMPT:

What was the God of your understanding in your childhood? Do you still look at that higher power, spirit, God in the same way or have you re-worked that power? Write a wanted Ad for the God of your desire.

This understanding of a new relationship with God, and also the courage to boldly have a voice with a less prevalent sense of fear came slowly. It was by no means overnight. It was to be a lifetime commitment. What a weight off my shoulders to fully believe that there is a cosmic spirit out in the Universe who knows more about my life and purpose than me. All that is required is to show up as my best self. When I started my journey of abuse recovery, and brought God onto my team, we had our hands full some days just keeping me in the game, never mind expecting joy, compassion and enlightenment. Over time, our work together has transformed. I awake ready for the gifts of my life, and occasionally I need to speak to God, close advisors, sponsors, about troubles in my wake. Almost 99% of the time, those troubles are of my old perceptions.

As I started to communicate with God, I wrote love letters to myself, and I expressed my deep joy and profound sorrow. I understood I didn't have to throw away all the parts of who I had been up to now to recover from abuse, but I could readdress the skills, desires and dreams that had been maligned by a life of suffering inside. To love myself and need that love. To be willing to take a leap that I could heal others with my words and my writing and my power of love for myself and others.

When I first faced the truth of the sexual abuse, I listened to Oprah's meditation series with Deepak Chopra. I also watched interviews with her on You Tube. Like millions of people around the world, I have a tremendous respect for Oprah's connection with her spirituality and intuition. I bought books she suggested like <u>Discover the Power Within You</u> by Eric Butterworth and <u>A Course in Miracles</u>. It was an interview she did at the Stanford Graduate School of Business that really hit home. She talked about Gary Zukov's <u>Seat of the Soul</u> and how vital it is for a person to change the way they think, and see themselves. To align with a deeper potential of the soul. She instructed us that we can get as much from our losses as our victories.

I downloaded Gary's book that night on my Kindle and couldn't put it down. As I read the chapters on intuition and the descriptions of the soul as a separate part of personality, I wondered what had been written about sexual abuse survivors and spirituality. I searched through the internet and a passage in a dissertation called "The Influence of Childhood Dissociative States from Sexual Abuse on the Adult Woman's Spiritual Development" by Cara Stiles, MSW, stuck with me. According to her research, the role of spiritual experiences for survivors in their lives was a highly unaddressed area in literature. My further interpretation was no one wanted to venture into the discussion with survivors about their higher power; a contentious subject based on what they had been through.

Yet having a spiritual force in your life was vital to face the horror ravaged on a childhood, and live a healthy adult life in the memories of the abuse. Most of my solutions in this book have evolved from a deeper relationship with God.

You can have no God or any God, but I believe to thrive as a sexual abuse survivor you do have to have some form of spiritual belief that can carry you on all the days, especially the rough days. Where you can fall to your knees, or the floor, or onto the sand of the beach, and hold yourself and know you are not alone because there is a power greater than yourself helping you through all this to blossom into the man or woman long hidden inside. In the quiet hours of writing, when the thoughts came front and center from a shame place such as: Who will ever want to marry me if I spew my dirty shameful secrets on the page? I knew it would be a man also walking a spiritual path directly towards me in the right time and space. I could have confidence in that belief despite appearances with a power greater than me.

WRITING PROMPTS:

What terrible thoughts about yourself can you lay for just a moment into the loving hands of another power that is your partner? Write some of those bad thoughts about yourself on paper, and hand them to your God. If you don't have one, hand them to the planet, the ocean. Just take in a partner in spirit who loves you.

About three years into sobriety and sexual abuse recovery, despite feeling like I had found God, I realized I was still not praying on my knees. Not to say God doesn't hear you unless you are on your knees, but in the inaction was a message of resistance waiting to be addressed.

"I can't pray on my knees," I said to my friend who had revealed he once struggled with reverence to God. "I feel like a Catholic and I am not one."

He explained his relationship with God radically changed when he added that extra piece of surrender.

Could I get on my knees before a God that had me go through decades just to get to a place to share my story?

I gave it a try, and when I prayed on my knees, I saw for the first time I held in my prayers the emotions of a disappointed little girl. I was praying to a child's God and that wasn't going to work for me as an adult. I saw I must set out to create an adult God. Suddenly I was liberated and felt like I had a new "God project." To show reverence to my partner in more miracles in the last four years than I had seen in a lifetime. God would also be on his knees to me. I must choose to see it.

WRITING PROMPT:

How do you pray? Even if you don't, write your own prayer that you could say every day for the best life for you.

God was not welcomed in my house after my grandfather converted from a Catholic to a born again Christian. My wonderful relationship with this man who I had sang show tunes with at the piano soured almost overnight. I was ten the last time we spoke. I called him about one of my school accomplishments.

"God did that, honey."

I was taken aback.

"No grandpa...I did."

I was happy to not talk to him after that because it was all about God. I had the best motive to do so. Where was God in my house full of abuse and secrets? People in my house were acting crazy by the mere act of behaving like NOTHING was going on. My young life was being twisted and warped in very conflicting ways and my grandfather was going on and on about how God creates all circumstances?

The crazy part about it was, my mom asked me in my twenties if my grandfather had ever abused me. I was horrified. I mean, what? It threw me off. I loved my grandfather. He made me laugh. He took me to piano lessons and after we had turkey dinners at the local steak house. I wonder if he abused her. We will never know, but it was just another layer of her denial when the abuse was happening right under her nose by her husband in her house.

WRITING PROMPT:

Was abuse ever brought up in your family before you were ready to face it? Even if it was indirect, write about what it felt like to have that subject come on the table even if it was off the mark.

I have attended Catholic churches in my lifetime for weddings or travel to Europe. I did have a profound experience at a memorial one year ago. The priest talked about death and all the times he has been with folks offering last rites and they have looked up to the sky and joy has been on their faces, and they knew right before they passed that the best was yet to come. Death is not the end of the journey he said, but the beginning. When abused as a small child, you experience an annihilation of your trust and our spirit. You die again and again. That is a sad thought, but as an adult, if you can take that concept and turn it into an almost out of worldly power, you are in fact so much more empowered than folks who have never stood at death's door.

You can walk out into the world and accomplish amazing feats because you have seen the worst of everyone's fears countless times. Turn misfortune into opportunity.

As an adult, I saw we were once powerless over the perpetrator and now to live a full adult life, we are asked as survivors to surrender and be powerless again? Tough call. God didn't protect us from the abuse. Or did he? It depends on your perspective of your whole life. You survived at the hands of a monster and are alive to tell about it and help another survivor. Isn't that the chain of service in the wheel of life? When abused in incest especially at the hands of a father, the ultimate provider, the key trusted family male, the survivor's life is lived with guarded caution and reality can take on frightening proportions. I numbed myself with marijuana incessantly. I was never safe and comfortable in any of my realities except when I was pregnant. "There is something wrong with me" is described as a sentiment a survivor feels in many self-help books.

It's not a great lightening bolt in the sky to surrender. With God's hand, we simply have to be willing to see the signs. As you grow into a bigger life where you believe you deserve way more than just pain and sorrow, you start to see the connections through others. I was growing into a brand as a book coach that scared the crap out of me because I was starting to own that I was intuitive and spiritual, and some of that had to do with the abuse. There was a plus side that one could apply to business? Woah. The day I admitted that to my branding coach I cried.

"I feel like I should put intuitive before my brand. But I am scared to actually tell people I think I have that level of spirituality. What if I don't?"

She told me it was very courageous and vulnerable to state this fact and that if I felt for sure that was what I was, then I needed to own it and put power behind it.

I did. What you water grows.

People do the work for your spiritual path through the direction of their God. It is complex and not fathomable by our small brains how this whole intricate system works. Your only work is to continue listening, showing up, surrendering so you can let God lead you to the people who answer your desires and prayers. God quickly shows me new paths when I don't even know I am ready. I ask God, but I don't always trust the cosmic infinite quantity of possibilities in the answers. I asked God when I knew I wanted to be an entrepreneur again what was I supposed to do for business? I knew it wasn't teaching in one classroom. I knew it wasn't movies. I did know there was a deep ache to guide people, lots of people, and to help them transform with stories. As a newly sober Alcoholic who some days could barely choose her socks, this was a daunting question to God. Yet, through others, he delivers.

I attended an AA meeting one year into sexual recovery in a real bad funk. The secretary approached me and asked if I could be the leader. I was baffled.

"I really have nothing illuminating to share this morning," I responded.

"No, you just read the format. We have a speaker," he said.

I agreed and stepped up onto the stage and sat down. Soon, in came the speaker Jay W., a big-hearted man with an even bigger personality. He is a death and grief coach. I introduced myself and within minutes he looked me right in the eyes and said, "You have what it takes to really be something. You need to call me. Let's talk."

I do believe that God had me at that meeting for a reason that morning so I called the card even with a slight worry he was hitting on me. Instead, after an hour on the phone with me, he introduced me to women writing and business coaches whose paths he had crossed in his work as a coach. I did not even know this world existed. All I had ever known was movies and parenting. I listened when he told me that I could be a writing coach but it wasn't easy to hear. No one told me those things. I reviewed the women on the list he had me jot down, and chose to attend a conference in Arizona for a business coach he highly referred. In a room with two hundred and fifty women entrepreneurs, my world was rocked and my life was forever changed. I stood up at a microphone and had a public cry with coach and hundreds of women. They understood my confusion and desire. I called Jay during one of the breaks, sobbing.

"I think I am going to sign up for a six month coaching program."

"That's wonderful," he said.

"But it's $5,000 and I have never invested that much money in me before and I am really scared." I felt like I was going to throw up. I couldn't breathe.

"I need you to take a few breaths, and then I want you to go to a quiet place, and I want you to ask God what he thinks you should do. I think you already know that this is something you want, and that scares you. You are worth it, Kim."

I hung up and all I needed was five minutes staring at the beautiful Arizona mountains surrounding the Ritz Carlton, the breeze ruffling my hair. I paid in full and shaking, re-joined the group.

"I signed up," I told the table of women where I was sitting.

"That's wonderful!" they said.

"I'm really scared," I revealed. Then the shaking started to subside because they held space for my courageous decision and they told me how they had done the same, and their businesses were thriving. I was no longer alone.

My old non-existent God was in a bottle of wine, a cigarette and resentment. God on that day was in all those women, Jay, the Arizona mountains, and me. I allowed it to be okay.

WRITING PROMPT:

Write out the story of when you took direction from someone where you had doubt but still followed through. Where did it lead you? How did you feel when you stretched out of your comfort zone?

About six months later, I transitioned into a life coaching program with a woman I met with such synchronicity, I couldn't discount God's hand. I didn't feel sick this time I paid which was progress, and I didn't need to ask anyone's advice. Later, though, I had a panic attack walking to "clear my head." All I did in that walk was spin out about how all this spending in a new business was going to financially ruin me. I felt a level of shame in the becoming of the new me. It was so painful to break out of the shell of the woman I had been masquerading as for so long. It was ripping me apart to make this next life up-level.

Returning from that walk, I sat on my stoop. I live in Los Angeles where it is hard to find places sound free but my street is deliciously quiet on Sundays. I heard the wind through the palm trees and realized it had been months since I had just sat on the stoop on a Sunday. I looked up into the palm fronds, the sun peeking through the breaks in a luminous shine, and noticed the browned leaves. I wanted to stop beating myself up. I didn't want to see death but something in me was dying. I felt a spiritual exhale.

I looked back up at the brown sticks and dry leaves and saw one of the branches was in fact not a dried up old plant but a brown little hummingbird. The shift in nature matched my exact shift in perfection, and it had revealed my totem animal. I knew this was not a mistake. God was sending me little signs that supported my new dream. You can see the world as a dried up old stick, or perhaps it is a vibrant busy little hummingbird.

WRITING PROMPT:

Where have you looked at a situation once in a negative way, and then had an experience where your perception was forced to shift. What did that feel like to witness?

Maya Angelou speaks of the importance of hours of aimless wandering. I grew up watching ants and looking for four leaf clovers. As I got caught up in the darkness of being an adult, and the loneliness I had not processed as a teenager, I perceived my wandering as lazy or careless. It was too painful to simply be with myself because I had no self. Today I have to wander even if it feels painful and awkward. I ignore every voice that questions whether I have the right to explore a new dress shop or walk into a bakery to try the samples. Fine, call me crazy hat lady but that chocolate cake is the bomb! God is in the spaces of wandering. I tune into his frequency and sure enough my intentions when I make a decision are crystal clear. Faith without works is dead. God wants to be a partner. He wants you to take action. Yet, you have to also listen to your heart. I get emotionally drained when my heart is shut down. No good manifestations can come in. When my heart closes down, my crazy head starts talking crap and I get scared especially when it is so loud. It takes a bit to quiet it down. I am no longer as afraid of those scared emotions because I have many tools to cope. I can lean into God and understand I may not know the truth. The same brain that created the problems is trying to figure out and solve the problems and that is a losing battle. The same brain that repressed the abuse for so long cannot be responsible for leading me to sanity! When I can sit in the stillness of silence every day, or I can simply be silent in a sea of people, I have a connected partnership with God and I feel alive.

WRITING PROMPT:

What prevents you from wandering? What would an ideal delicious day of wandering look like for you? Write it down, the actions, the surrender, with detail and imagination and post it on your wall. Then one day, go do it!

Considering something better for myself is definitely in a partnership with God and as I mentioned it can come through other people. There are messengers and they don't necessarily belong to a church or religious entity. My God doesn't belong to any entity than the earth and the sun and sky for me. It is okay to exude and expand my big energy with people in a safe space, and to moderate my energy with folks I am skeptical about. God gives me permission to do that. Eventually "spiritual reboots" became a part of my schedule. What is a "spiritual reboot?" It is unique to everyone, and I urge you to make your list. To help you along, I have listed mine:

1. A good night's sleep after a conversation with God.
2. Morning prayer followed by open eye meditation practice.
3. Dressing nice for an event I don't want to attend. If I make a new contact, or have a good time that is a turbo re-boot, but going can be enough.
4. Asking someone about their health, job or any current situation, and not talking about myself at all.
5. Attentive time blocks with my kids when I don't look at my phone.
6. Dancing free form to music either in the house or in a venue.
7. Finding gratitude in my romantic relationship outside my expectations.
8. Playtime with a friend

WRITING PROMPTS:
What are your spiritual reboots? Write them down.

Some of these may seem like obvious actions, but for me, when I am headed towards isolation or the old patterns of thinking, they become weird and scary. I had to believe the time was needed for them for "my life success" overall. They were part of my "new religion." They were essential part of my success. I was crafting a new life. At the beginning of this journey of coming to terms with sexual abuse three years ago and concurrently writing this book. I met women who, like me, entered twelve step programs because they knew something was "really wrong with them" beyond their childhood suffering, and along the way encountered that raw anxiety when you start to face your fears and change yourself on a cellular level. Many of these women were able to vocalize the sexual abuse but they needed more spirituality to get them to the next stage in their lives. Twelve step meetings became that safe place to contemplate a power greater than themselves outside the church that was soiled by what went on silently (or maybe not so silently but violently) in their homes.

They needed to talk about the voices that said things like, "You reveal too much. These are our secrets." Or "You are just looking for attention." Or "You spend too much time on self transformation. You are reckless and impetuous. You are a silly foolish little girl. If you just did what you were told and stopped stirring up the pot of life, you would survive." It's a challenge to tell those voices to fuck off but I learned to say, "What if everything is working out exactly the way it is supposed to?" That calms me right down.

WRITING PROMPT:

What voices do you need to silence? How can turning to your spiritual re-boots distract you from them if you can't quiet them down?

There is a desire to have a deepening connection to God, a desperation to know that God is fundamentally available and not just a figment of our imagination as we strip away the layers of the self that we shaped as survivors and the new self which is shiny and clean and evolved and raw and real. To not go back, we need to reach for a more tangible God we had or didn't have as children. This "God" can be for you a drawing, a sculpture, an alter, a Buddha, it has so many possibilities. But we all need something. I know that for some of you, that is a courageous step because as survivors, we have major trust issues. I know I am acutely aware of my desire to see someone

I am starting to trust in a dark light soon so I can sever the further growth of trust. That would be crazy vulnerable because what may I say or do next?

When our identity is not grounded in a spiritual belief system, we cling to other people co-dependently and because we are abuse survivors, we cling to the wrong people. People who will re-enact for us the same dynamics we experienced in the titilation and then abandonment of the abuse. My dad would come and go at night, and I never knew when or how the abuse would happen. There was an uncertainty I grew up with about people's permanence. It is hard for me to cope with elusive people. I can't have them in my life.

Everyone has a different scenario and choices for their spiritual solutions. People have physical and geographical limitations to how much access they have to a spiritual community. For me, living in the moment happens with a strong presence of spiritual support because I need that hole hollowed out of my soul by the abuse filled by good stuff. When we were being abused, the reality of the moment, of what was happening was so severe and frightening, we left the moment to cope. It's called disassociation, but I call it "jumping out of my body." We were there, and we were aware, we had our physical bodies there which were reacting either positively or negatively or both simultaneously, but we had checked out as a coping mechanism. I also realized that this was where I jumped into other people's bodies. It's hard to explain what that means but I was excited to discover this concept and apply it as an intuitive book coach. I could sense with my open heart chakras and tingles in my legs when someone was really writing and speaking from their most authentic truth. Now I see this ability to leave my body, to use my body to accept other's pain and stories as gifts very unique to abuse survivors. A part of our own spiritual make-up. A wonderful sense of intuition and an almost psychic capability that was created in the disassociation we experienced in the abuse. The leaving of our body is profound.

The core of spirituality is perspective. Surviving abuse is only one part of my story. It is not my whole story. I have so many parts to myself that can thrive and grow. The "dirty little secret" of abuse is no longer a secret but one of the realities of my past. I get clearer every day how it affected me but I move closer to the positive when I unwilling to feed into my negative perspective. I have had a powerful and amazing perception available to me my whole life, I just didn't know how to access it.

You can find your spirituality and God in any place that works for you. Spirituality can be in the rustling of the trees and the crashing ocean. You don't have to travel to Peru or go meditate for 45 silent minutes to connect with your higher power. When life gets convoluted and warped for me today, I seek the simplicity of the trees. Their movement and sound is where I go back to my soul.

WRITING PROMPT:
Where do you find spirituality when you need to connect?

CHAPTER SIXTEEN
TAKING BACK MY BODY

Many people who suffered childhood abuse destroy their bodies with anorexia, bulimia, binging, and obsessing over food to the point where they are distracted and checked out of their lives, their vision and their purpose. I tried bulimia for about two weeks when I was fifteen, and the sheer act of vomiting, drooling into a toilet bowl, tears streaming down my face, struck me as way too much work. So I never did it again unless I was super drunk and spinning. Then I had no problem jamming three fingers down in my throat to get all the alcohol out. Why go to bed loaded with an upset stomach when you know how to induce vomiting, right? I was always a practical girl.

The act of eating and then exercising the calories off was a big part of keeping my inner self from facing the sexual abuse. I never became overweight due to vigilance of body image. Being fit kept me attractive to men and worthy despite hating myself inside. It was a cycle of distraction and obsession. In recovery, I surrendered to food as a friend, a nutrient, a social catalyst, a dating construct, a guilty pleasure, or occasional crutch, and eliminated old attachments of trauma to food. Food comes from this earth, our soil, nature, and abundance, and to cut oneself off can be cutting you off to the whole epicenter of self. I found a freedom with food, and nourished my body for function so I could go after a bigger life. It was no surprise I was the Editor of a food journal while coping with abuse in the early days, learning about the origins of food and the distribution channels to supermarkets, and then to actually work at a supermarket, experiencing the distribution of food, as well as the customers who bought food, and why. God puts us exactly where we need to be to support our lessons, transformation and growth. The mental energy and process of food. I recall lovers coming in to Trader Joes shopping together, their food lists emblems of their devotion to each other. Cooing at each other at check out, pleased they would be communing together over this food in love. I did do the shopping and cooking with a few men, but it lacked that luster of love because it was not yet within me. The love of self was not there, so making a nice meal was just like a falsity on top of it. It took four years, but I am with a man who I now cuddle with at check stands. He adores me, and makes food for me, and I eat it with no obsession about weight.

I did go to one Survivors of Incest Anonymous meeting and they were all enormously overweight and clutching stuffed animals. I can't say I know if this is the case for all chapters, but for this one, I said to myself, I am not going down with that ship. I did share my story publically for the first time to them, and by the grace of God they held fantastic space, but I did not go back. They did not have what I wanted. I don't want to be gorging myself on food and clutching a stuffed animal as a sexual abuse survivor. I am making no judgment, but the identification was not for me. I want to be physically healthy, aligned and free to live in my history.

Two years into recovery from sexual abuse, I stumbled upon a way abandonment from my dad, loneliness, food and men all connected. It was a reenactment I had engaged in for years. It came about when I was asked by my branding coach to write a power story. I had written many of these in various speeches for my coaching business, as well as on my web site so I felt like I expulsed everything involving a story I would feel comfortable to tell for branding.

"What do I write?" I asked her. "I feel like I have written it all a few times at least."

"Just open yourself up and write. See what comes up," she said.

I pondered this while boiling a hot dog in my kitchen. My fridge notoriously becomes a barren wasteland when my kids go out of town for a week after Christmas or during spring break. We are talking one stick of butter, a sad slab of tofu, browning basil and mustard/mayo. So I was eating what was remaining, which was a hot dog that I had justified as "organic" and I was adding it to a scrambled egg. I'm nouveau I told myself. Some restaurant out there is using the humble hot dog in dishes and getting accolades for it. But as I stood by the boiling pot of water, I was flashed back to my dad's kitchen as a teenager. The deep loneliness of having only hot dogs to boil in a soundless kitchen of a second floor apartment in Rhode Island at 16. I recalled the silence and the foreboding emptiness and absence of anyone to talk to. No one to speak with, swap stories, comment on the weather, school, whether I was happy or sad. I watched my teen age self cross the slanted linoleum of that kitchen, the hot dog now in a bun, on a plate, and sit at the table. There was not a parent to be found. It was a nefarious neglect. I was left with $20 for the weekend, but no car and no plan. I wasn't given the tools for survival, never mind how to be a sexual abuse survivor in the home of my perpetrator.

I decided then I deserved nothing.

That teenage girl didn't even know what to wish for, only to awkwardly stand in what she was given. She would squeeze ketchup on the hot dog and sit at the table with two chairs and eat slowly, methodically. Chewing the only sound.

WRITING PROMPT:

Write a memory in your youth involving food. What were the circumstances, and why do you remember this particular meal? Who was it with? See what comes forth in the writing.

I married men who would feed me. They could not feed my soul, because that was impossible. There was a fortress around it I couldn't even access. My in-laws would wine and dine me; crab and shrimp on the deck of a Eastern seaboard summer home, oysters and champagne over the San Francisco Bay. If they fed me, I would be fine. Yet, it was never enough to surmount the dark, sad loneliness of a little girl left alone with no money and no food for weekends when she needed a father, and a mother, the most.

I also post marriages dated men for food. This would have been a good patch job for the hole of loneliness and avoidance of sexual abuse recovery but God had another plan. Remember that therapist who came on to me that I thought was boyfriend material? I was with him when I got on a foot fungus medication. The fungus had been plaguing me for five years and it was time to deal. The doctor had two conditions with the medicine. One, I couldn't drink for a year because it is very taxing to my liver, and two, I would eventually lose taste for a while.

I was in a complete panic.

"For a foot fungus? Like how much no drinking?" I asked. The doctor eyed me cautiously.

"Well, no drinking means no drinking."

I shook my head. "Not going to happen, but I'll try."

"Okkkkaaayyy... "she said.

The food lost taste one morning. I woke up and nothing had flavor. I was with this man for fine dining and fucking. Now when we went out for really nice dinners, I couldn't taste anything. My best thinking was not to evaluate this useless relationship or question why it was so profoundly hard to stay away from wine. It was to use this opportunity to get skinnier.

I did eventually break up with him. I finally realized he was disrespectful. A year later I started choking from Achalasia, and that kicked off a whole other part of this food journey.

Today I remind myself to love my body as it carries my soul. I can be that woman who other abuse survivors can look at and see as examples of courage, self love and liking my insides as much as my outsides... even when I have days where I don't like what is happening to my body. I am in heels and a blue dress that shimmers on my body as I dance in the club with wild abandon to the perfect music. With all I have been through in the last four years, I am not the same girl who maniacally works out any more. Instead I look at my schedule, packed with serving amazing book clients, picking my kids up from school and hanging out with them, going on dates, my own writing, never mind a pretty rigorous meditation practice, and there is no longer time for fifteen mile runs. So while I am not a string bean anymore, I can still wear a bathing suit at the beach without being horrified at myself. Being as skinny as I can be is no longer a life goal to prove my value.

Someone once said to me, "If my mind didn't need my body to carry it around, it would have killed it long ago." You are working on your new thinking and vision as you recover. You will need a strong body to transport you to help others and love with a boundless capacity. You have worked on your mind, now it is time to work on the container.

I can't achieve new heights of awareness if I am caught in the food/exercise self-loathing distraction paradigm. This awareness is challenging at times because my brain wants to tell me I am getting fatter, and no one will love me. You can tell that voice that whoever only loves you for your body is a shallow mother fucker and you should kick he or she to the curb! Do you want to be happy and less hard on yourself with larger love handles or do you want to be intensely focused on your outsides leading to more desperation for those hole fillers like any man who leers at you. I don't want anyone to ever take my power away again. They can't if I am fit in my thinking before my figure. With safety, awareness, recovery and God, you will grow to be beautiful in ways you never thought possible. In a heart centered soul way.

WRITING PROMPT:

What kind of dialogue about your body happens when you are achieving new goals? Do you find you check out of your reality to obsess over body, or eat anxiously in order to disconnect from your soul? Write out one of these dialogues.

Food can be escapism from facing abuse, recovering from abuse and stepping into a bigger life. Just when you are about to have that incredible profound creative or personal experience that explains so much, you have to go suddenly snack. I am vigilant about escapism but also kind to myself. I catch myself wandering into the kitchen for yogurt covered pretzels right when I was on the cusp of a serious personal breakthrough. It got a little too intimate in the head-heart connection. It's okay if this occurs for you. Just slow down and accept. Reconnect in a nonpunishing way to your spirit. Luckily my bout with Achalasia where I was distinctly choking for a year left behind a ghost pang in my throat that acts up when I am shoving food in unconsciously or eating faster than I am swallowing or digesting. It's my doorbell to God. God is in my food issues with me. There is NO area of my life that God isn't interested in hearing my prayers and helping me if I am willing to be helped. I can breathe and make a decision even while that bag of chocolate chips is clutched in my hand. I may know it would feel so good to fill my mouth with chocolate but I ask God to show me how I don't need these addictions, these false attractions, that later will put me in the tail spin of I am not skinny enough, I need to go walk for an hour because I couldn't stop eating … I need to take time away from my carefully laid plans to alleviate the guilt of the chocolate chips when I could've prayed and not eaten them at all.

So I started exploring how to be profound about the food I eat. Who am I eating it with, and what is that experience? Is that meal a choice or is it an old pattern of men taking care of me? Is it a meal with a friend, and if so, do I need to overstuff myself due to anxiety of the day, or can I share safely with this person. Can I find a healthier outlet for food that I am eating?

WRITING PROMPT:

Write about a great meal you had lately and who you had it with. Were you comfortable with the amount you were eating and the conversation?

My relationship with food is connected to my self-love. I don't ever have to beat myself up or make myself feel like crap if I ate too much cake. I am learning it is cyclical. PMS and my menstrual cycle or how much sleep I have had affects when I eat and what I crave. There is normalcy here that happens to almost all women in my age group, and they haven't been necessarily abused. I don't think straight at my age when I am tired, and not thinking straight means "I am not enough" which leads to gorging on food, particularly the chocolate almond and yogurt covered pretzel self serve bins at Ralphs. I need to engage in conscious contact with the act of the food going up to my mouth, tasting the food and swallowing it. If only we all took the time to look at the food we toss into our carts at the supermarket and think about where it came from, who packaged it, what it costs, and the act in which you will partake in when eating it. Did I ever think lovingly about my digestive system besides an assumption it needed to keep chugging along to accept all the pot smoke, and cigarettes, alcohol and vitriol and rage I poured down it? How unkind I was to my insides. I have used consumption in my to bury my sexual abuse trauma.

I jammed my system full of food, drink and exercise so that I could block the channels that could bring forth the words from my heart.

When I first started sexual abuse counseling, I begged my therapist to make sure I didn't get fat. That was a huge fear of mine. Even though one part of me knew that I could stay fit by hiking, yoga, and the occasional walk around the block, it could no longer be to attract a man so I felt worthy. The fight continued in my mind for a long time. Aren't men attracted to women by sight first and then they fall in love, my mind fought me. So if you are flabby, and not toned and gorgeous, you won't have a great pick of guys. Then I thought about the pick of guys I got into relationships with in my pre-recovery mindset. Guys who wouldn't tell me they loved me, but their penis loved me. Hooray for that! They were not attracted to me for the essence of my heart but I didn't have that connection for me yet. They liked my traumatized self. While the sex was consistent, I would orgasm more than often as a performance. I was a great performance artist. There was no mind-body connection.

WRITING PROMPT:

What kind of men or women do you hope to attract as the recovering you? How do you see your body in their eyes? To understand this, you need to write a body map. Take a minute to write about some of your favorite body parts and why you love them.

I believe in body memory, and on a cellular level, my body was condensed with a lifetime of trauma and external validation. It had survived this long as a mass that took in stuff that was foreign and not good for it, and now my mind was giving it messages there were going to be some changes coming. I wanted to change the way I appreciated this body that carried my heart.

Once I started to love the body that was mine, I wanted to wear different clothes in a new way. Brighter colors and styles. I had always just clothed the body to get to where I needed to go. I often looked good because I am a survivor and I can fake it on the exterior really well. When I took a voluntary position of service in my first year of sobriety greeting people at the door at a very popular AA speaker meeting, I had to suit up. People would be all glam. It was a who's who of the west side. We would even get some celebrities. So I forced myself to clean up for this position every Sunday I didn't have my kids, and greet people. Part of being of service was to make sure my appearance matched who I was aspiring to become. Regardless of loathing of body image or the deformity I felt inside. Sure, I liked looking hot for some guys who paid attention to me, but I was shedding that addictive layer gradually in that time and in that service. I was not staying home in sweats eating chocolate chips. You can do this too … put your face on your new self and seek recovery actively from abuse in the simple act of suiting up and showing up. The voices would say to me, "You live in lack, you aren't exercising enough so why even try to look or feel like healthy successful people?" I would respond, "Fuck you voices," and get dressed in suitable clothes to stand at that AA meeting door and greet. Later the voices said, "You win. You are changing."

WRITING PROMPT:

Where can you show up today dressed your best, even if your head tells you that you are not enough? Write about what would happen if you went there? Get your worst fears out on paper, don't hold back! You need to see how silly those fears are, and it may be some very imaginative writing to boot!

So what does one do if they are in the perpetual state of crisis of unfolding their sexual abuse trauma, and using food to assuage the demons inside? Write fifty times "Food won't fill my hole." The perfect road is never a straight line in any of this work. I have overeaten with far less shame because I see the progress within myself. I'm not going to change everything in four years what was in place for the first forty-three years. Deepak did a whole meditation series on being conscious of what we are putting in our bodies and that includes men! I can choose how and what I eat every day and who I have sex with. Eating slow can be silent, connected, and in gratitude. Making love with your soul mate can be the same.

Today, I am in acceptance that God will show me each day what foods I need to nourish my body alongside the sleep I need, the self care, and the people I am drawn to connect with that I can empower and learn from. I love holistic practitioners who care about food and the body/mind connection. I understand that all around me are a million options for food. Every corner you go on, food is sold. I can know that I never will have to go hungry. That in itself is wonderful relief. When I don't think about my body and food obsessively, I have more time to think about others in my life, and how I can help people. I get out of a selfish victim place and outwardly nourish. I say this all the time in this book, but we are powerful as abuse survivors. We have strong courageous voices. Think about what you could accomplish as a change agent if you spent even one-third of the time food obsessing helping to solve global problems?

WRITING PROMPT:

How can you turn your food obsessions into positive thinking today? Where can you take the obsessive thinking about food or men and turn it into brain power for solving problems in your community, your family, or even the world? For fun, write out a manifesto of what you would change in your world.

Don't get me wrong. I am far from the Mother Theresa of food. I still periodically have moments of checking out by shoving nuts or popcorn in my face while standing in my kitchen lost in some fearful spiral or obsession when I could be engaging in horse play with my children, reading a good book or stretching and meditating. Sometimes I have great clarity and health, and some days I am confused and addictive but I am never back to where I was when I was denying abuse. The good news is, the more distance you have from the initial shock of facing sexual abuse, the more you see the change you can make in the world with your vision, and the less you beat yourself up with food.

You don't waste time fighting food anymore because you have gotten busy with your life.

CHAPTER SEVENTEEN
SLOWING IT ALL DOWN

I have always been a fast mover and high achiever. I get up at 5:30 AM and I do about six hundred things a day. Not every day, but many days. My warped perception of self did not allow me to acknowledge that I was a success so I had to always push myself harder so I never really took in and tasted the essence of what I was experiencing. It was the runner mentality I had in denial. If I don't keep moving, then I will have to think about how I know deep down inside there is something I am supposed to face.

My life was about going after grandiose high stakes and big splashes. No simple life affirming joys allowed. Today I am aware that when I allow there to be space in between my activities, I have epiphanies and solutions that would be impossible to gage a year ago. Slowing down on a daily basis to re-focus your intentions on heart-centered actions can cause panic at first. The scared and uncomfortable feelings are a new experience because you are facing them without secrets. You can lean on the simple concept that everything is exactly all right just as it is. You are recovering, and your whole life as you know it will change. About a year into sexual abuse healing, I needed to walk around hearing unji yoga breathing in the back of my throat. It would center me. There were days the breathing would sound so loud I would be able to tune out all the other invading noises so I could stay centered and calm. It would remind me I am human being and I am on this earth breathing. Everything else is extra. Everything else is function.

Slowing down and allowing the presence of God to speak through me has been one of the biggest learning curves in my recovery. Lying still while caressed by a parent inappropriately makes stopping and allowing yourself to be open very challenging but when you get to the other side of it, it's beautiful. I try to be present for each interaction but I also don't need to understand or even clarify joy. I hear the little miracles from messengers – people in my life to guide me for a minute, an hour, or longer. If I wasn't that young girl trying to always figure out when and how about abuse, or silent scorn or witnessing angry adults not able to manage their own damaged childhoods, I may have had some bandwidth to start to ask Who am I? Now I can, and it's not too late. It is not too late for you, no matter what age you start to face sexual abuse. The quality of the moments when you step into the new power of the recovered you blow decades of a false angry repressed self out of the water.

WRITING PROMPT:

Is it easy for you to be still and slow down? Write about rushing around and forcing solutions. Where do you feel that in your body when you write about "making shit happen."

When I force others to make fast decisions, and press solutions and outcomes, I get ahead of my mind, my body, and I fall into old patterns of trauma. I doubt, panic, judge and get overcome by intense sadness. I think I am a crappy piece of shit. I punish myself. Yes, I do this sometimes even today, and I can imagine as life gets bigger and more complex in all the fruitful ways, I will have many more bouts of rushing forward to manage. I can't explain why but the slower my world gets the faster the desires I have flow towards me. My life has a luscious velocity that is scintillatingly slow. What a paradox!

Let me give you an example with a dirty window. I live in a perfectly nice apartment, with a kitchen window that looks out onto a small parking lot. Nothing glamorous but I can see the sunset and the moon rise. The window got very dirty from the smog of the various cars coming in and out of the lot, and about two years ago, fed up at the obstruction of my view, I decided to clean it. Nothing in my life at this time was done with ease and grace, so I only did a quick evaluation of the two panes of glass, didn't walk outside, and used my best thinking to duct tape a sponge on the end of a mop head and jam it in between the two panes of glass. My kids, hearing my tone of voice and aggressive determination, steered clear of the whole operation. All I ended up with was a six inch clean circle and a sponge stuck between the glass panes. I decided that I had proved to myself what I already knew... I deserved to only have a small circle to look through as I was still a dirty girl. Yet I had learned enough self-love to surrender to there not being a solution at the moment. Six months later, and a lot of profound abuse recovery miles logged, I was returning from a lovely Sunday outing at the Farmer's Market. I had gotten used to asking myself What Makes Me Happy? On this particular morning, the voice replied, "Clean that darn window!" Within seconds, I had a Swiffer wet mop and a stool, and went outside to easily wash the window. I saw the difference in this example of how I approached challenges, believing I deserved what made me happy and therefore the Universe would provide the answers. That window turned out sparkling and for the first time since I had moved in, I could see the trees and the sky. I had not cleaned just a dirty window that day, but an old story. The only person who made it hard and impossible was the woman who couldn't calm down long enough to believe she deserved happiness.

WRITING PROMPT:

Is there a circumstance where you tried to force an outcome and had to walk away with a false belief you didn't deserve happiness? Did you return to the scenario? If not why? Write about how you could approach the situation differently.

Deserving happiness frees me from anger, and provides me the capacity to cope with the greater world as a woman who believes in herself. It takes time to learn that life wants the best for you. You just need to keep showing up and believing. You will feel anger severing ties to old dysfunctional crutches like I never get what's due to me, but it is just a letting go of what made you feel falsely safe.

These lessons continue to come to me on different planes of maturity. I need to believe I not only deserve happiness, but that I can say No to what I do not think will offer me that state of mind. Slowing down I can make smarter less impulsive decisions with money. I forget that God has my back and that I am an over achiever. What a delicious combination! What gets me really thrown off is when I allow emotion to overtake me. I am suddenly that little girl who never was allowed self-expression, so I lunge at things to fix me so I don't have to sit in any discomfort. Slowing down forces us to sit in discomfort and trust.

Slowing down with my children has been the most incremental lesson I could learn because I have a knee jerk reaction still with aggression. If I am lonely or tired, and have been single parenting intensely without a break, I will have adult temper tantrums. Then my soul hurts as I feel my children's disappointment and sadness. They need me there for them. Not some sniveling little inner child who has not been seen or heard. This alone is a purpose to slow down.

My daughter did not get into student council and she was really angry and uncomfortable about it. It was a lot of raw unbridled energy in the car the day I picked her up. She snarled instead of speaking. It stretched my bounds of understanding and my capacity to just allow there to be quiet safe space for her but I told myself that time felt to me a lot longer because of my emotional composition, and that she would find her recovery on her own pace. She did, and I was there for her to hold the space. When my seven year old falls down and is bruised, it is very hard for her to accept any kind of concern about her well being. She has built a bit of a protective wall around herself, perhaps because of the unstable turmoil when she was two. My capacity to accept this behavior, which could or could not be because of me being so shut down when she was very little, is so big now that I find ways to touch her and soothe her when she is least resistant. I rub and scratch her back at bedtime or I make sure if we are out somewhere that I rub her arm, hug her. It is beautiful that we kiss on the lips and connect and we tell each other we love each other.

WRITING PROMPT:

Write about a day you honored space for someone who was struggling, and what that did for your sense of personal character. Alternatively, you can write about a day you were not able to hold space for a person who needed you, and your opinions on yourself looking back.

I dated a man late last year who used the word 'capacity' when I shared I was at my limit in dealing with an issue with one of my kids.

"You have a capacity," he said. "And you reached it."

I would have felt his comment was judgmental if I didn't know that he too shared a disappointing relationship with a father.

"My father did not do the one job necessary; protect me as a kid," he told me one day in a rare vulnerable moment.

Our two stars had aligned to date, even just for a few months, because we were healing souls finding adulthood after pain from our fathers. Therefore his message about capacity had impact with me. It forced me (even with a little 'I'll show him') to lean in to the next level of life expansion with my kids, and show up in a more mature way. He was one of many messengers we can allow in our lives when we slow down.

As women, society has instructed us to stretch our capacity. Make equal pay, show up equal time but continue to take on the more extensive tasks of child rearing and running a home. It is smart for abuse survivors to find a support system for these tasks if they cannot get traction from their husbands so they don't reach maximum capacity in a negative way. That will bring up the feelings of being used and extended and there will be untethered anger that can be damaging. We can be newly birthed women with businesses we love, connection and involvement with our children, lovers or a romantic partner, high incomes...if we know the limits of our capacity doing it solo and enlist help. People in my life who I have cared for have pushed me to see I had more emotional capacity in a kinder gentler way than I would ever give myself credit for. When I give myself the permission to be happy and seek that which makes me happy, I don't need so much capacity because I am not extending myself all over the place for objectives or goals that are not with my new highest alignment.

WRITING PROMPT:

Who in your life supports you during your recovery from sexual abuse? Who has come into your life as a messenger, even for a brief period of time, to teach you that you have more capacity for life than you were giving yourself credit for?

Sex and love addiction was always under the surface for me, but it swooped in with a gusto as I got closer to unearthing the lie about the abuse. It made its exit slowly. Letting go of hiding my feelings behind the mechanics of sex is not a short order. I had nestled a long time in the abusive space of being a body. I had another incident that was a turning point in truly honoring who I was today in my body. Starting my business, I had a very small income the first year. I qualified for Medi-Cal and they pick your doctors. The primary doctor you are assigned recommends you to a system that spits out an assignment for an OB/Gyn. I drove 40 minutes to a doctor who, bless her heart, served young unwed low-income pregnant mothers. As I sat in the waiting room for my annual pap, I felt shame about my income, my status, but I also fought my ego to say, it's okay for today if this is where I am at. This is not about whether I am better or worse off than anyone. I thanked the Universe for free health care. I expressed gratitude to America. I worked whatever I had to keep me in a positive mind frame.

I went back in an attempt to get an IUD, but we couldn't negotiate a safe enough space for me to relax for the insertion. Then a strange rash appeared on my upper thighs. My first thought (even though I had safe sex with the last partner) was something like sca-bies or an STD. I was back to dirty girl. I called her office and they were not receptive to treating a potential scabies situation because of the highly infectious nature, and it could get on the babies. I was pissed but not about their reaction or the rash. I knew, even if it was free and low income, I deserved different care at a place that served a 47 year old woman no longer having babies. Also why was I driving 40 minutes when I live in Los Angeles with a zillion women doctors? I was pissed because I had put up with less in telling myself that was my value. I waited for my anger to pass, and then with ease, I called the multiple chains of numbers at Medi-Cal. Each time I was bumped to a new representative, I repeated the mantra, "I am not getting the care I require as a 47 year old woman no longer having babies and I would like a change." I received a new doctor only 5 miles away that dealt with women in my age range. It took me nine months to make this call, and the change happened in seven minutes.

WRITING PROMPT:

If there is any action you are frustrated with and continuing to do in defeat, ask yourself what would make you happy in that situation? Then let it sit until you can find a solution with a clear voice or action, and ease and flow. Write out what these situations are. That helps with clarity.

I hate to break this to you especially if you, like me, think multi tasking will get you to where you hope to go. There is no grace in fourteen balls in the air, especially after surmounting sexual abuse. Why after I lived a life disconnected from the sweet soul center of my body and soul because I harbored the secret of abuse would I want to drive myself crazy juggling a conference call while my nails dry cooking pasta for the kids and obsessing over a camp site I need to book? That was how I lived my whole life until recovery. Go on high octane, and then burn out stoned on the couch. I was in extremes all the time. I never believed there was enough time to get done everything I needed to do in life for success. Yet I wasn't even living a true life. I was in a lie. So I did a million transitions and tasks a day and then struggled with the fact that I didn't seem to have any space to think or process. I knew that I needed to shut off that message I heard for so long: "Women are excellent multi taskers, more so than men." I took on the multi tasking role as a mother because that is what is expected, but really if you think about it, curling my hair, making my kids' lunches, drinking coffee and checking email all at the same time does not set my day off to a very focused start. I began to wonder what it would be like if I took each task at a time. Who told me I wasn't allowed? I decided to give it a try and ironically, I would leave the house earlier and calmer. Here is why: the more I do, the more my brain wants to do because it is addicted with being filled with stuff so I can't get to the real heart of my feelings and thoughts that will foster a connection with myself and others. It is better to be alone in the commotion and busy than truly in my precious heart wanderings. When I stay in one place, and tell my mind, it is okay to be in this one place, my ego fights me. It tells me silence is dangerous and scary. My state of consciousness when I was being abused was survive the silence. Now I am learning how to embrace the silence. The beauty of my soul with my own moments in time. Sometimes those moments are shared with others. It will be a life long practice to listen to what makes me happy in any moment and go for it without thinking I am a loafer or a side stepper or an addict.

WRITING PROMPT:

What is your relationship with silence? Write a story about an experience with silence. It can be positive or negative, and you can be the main character or you can fictionalize.

The secret is the richer and fuller your life gets, everything is actually moving faster. The decisions to be in abundance, believing, potential and possibility are always in calm spaces. That slow believing brings what you desire to manifest to you at rapid speeds. When opportunity knocks, I can say "Yes!" quickly without feeling like I am engulfing myself with unnecessary space filling commitments. I am on this planet to be fully present in anything I am doing and enjoy the speed in which I set the clock.

WRITING PROMPT:

Keep a journal of hour by hour what you did every day for a week. At the end of the week find a moment where the only action you will take is to read the journal. Don't read the journal while waiting for a phone call or something is baking in the oven … purposely make the time to just read and see what makes you happy that you did, and what creates a sense of frustration. Start to do more of the happy acts and see where your life unfolds.

It won't always be easy. You will want to rebel. That is when your faith in slowing down has to be the strongest. Talk to people you love and trust about the discomfort. I confessed to my boyfriend while lying in bed on a romantic getaway that after an intense day together I was feeling like I had to "get out," and "run." I was in the old thinking that if there was a good build up of intimacy, like his devoted attention, that silence would disintegrate everything. I will be forgotten and left. I would disappear and no one would notice. I would be obliterated by the silence; purged of every raw essence of me and left splayed. Once I shared with him, it diffused the desire and we were closer than ever. I got to spend the next hour in intimacy with him, instead of off in my old programming of self-preservation. I can't go there anymore because I am no longer in denial.

Once I shared that, it diffused the desire and we were closer than ever. I got to spend the next hour in intimacy with him, instead of off in my old programming of self-preservation. I can't go there anymore because I am no longer in denial.

My dad may have stolen my innocence from me but my journey is to see that in a natural rational world, people simply come and go. There is silence. As abused kids, we fold into our abuser's identity and cannot imagine we have our own. We cling to the identities of our lovers, friends and professions.

In slow action, there can be silence where that all the shifts can occur. As you heal, you are reconciling the adult from the child, the longing from the abuser, and slowly feeling your way into your present life.

CHAPTER EIGHTEEN
CHANGING ROMANTIC LOVE

W e need to address romantic love just like Salt-n-Pepa had to talk about sex. For many abuse survivors, it is a big ick. Learning to love you is hard enough never mind another person in a romantic way. We deserve to have the best in all areas of our lives, and the deepest partnership one can achieve in love provides some of the most necessary healing. Especially when it is free of the ties of addiction and codependence.

While writing this chapter, I had a profound and scary dream about the lock on the bedroom door in my dad's house as a teen. It was one of those dreams where you wake up still in the dream in a state of panic, anxiety and fear. I knew as the dreaming teenage Kim I had to get my clothes out of the dresser drawer and run because the lock on the door was jiggling. Someone wanted in ... bad. I woke up finally from this dream and went for a run to shake it off. On the run, pausing on the corner for a red light, I had an epiphany ... my dad had been in love with me. Not the good kind of healthy and safe father and daughter love that I know exists between my kids and their dad, but the twisted wrong love. I flashed back to one night in my junior year in high school, I was living with him, and had that lock on the inside of my bedroom door. I don't recall now if he put it there for me, or if I asked for it, but it existed. I had locked it and snuck out to meet my friend. We didn't do anything wrong, just drove around the deserted streets of Warren, Rhode Island in her convertible. Bored to hell like most of my teenage years when

I wasn't doing mushrooms, mescaline or drinking profusely. Then she dropped me off. When I got back-and for decades and decades this connection alluded me-my dad had lined up all my stuffed animals by the outside front door indicating I was caught. My heart sunk and I recall then as my young self thinking it was funny and twisted at the same time. Today, as the adult Kim standing on the street, I realized this was exactly how my stuffed animals used to be lined up on either side of me in my bed as a child. They were my protectors but they were no defense against his visits, no matter what their strength in formation. This macabre stuffed animal congregation outside the front door was almost exact to the line up of my childhood bed (except I had less stuffed animals at 15 than at 8). I never questioned why he was trying to get in my room late at night as a teen, or how he knew I was out.

It was a staggering realization that his message that night was "How dare you abandon me. How dare you not want to return my love in this way?" He was saying he was in love with me in a very sick and unhealthy way a man should not be in love with his daughter. My relationship with him growing up was like a wife. We went on outings to all kinds of places, and he and my mom never went on dates. He had sexual expression with me that I assume he did not have with her. Then I got older and would rebel against my mom and move in with him because I thought that was what I was supposed to do. Classic return to the abuser. For a long time I hated my mom for a childhood of repressing my feelings and rage. I didn't know the extent of the secrets in my house. I had blocked it all out. Could she have saved me? Not sure. It's too long ago now to know. Living with my dad as a teen, the abuse changed to neglect. He would leave me alone on weekends with nothing. No food, no support. Nothing. He would abandon me. You don't want to love me. You don't want to give me what I want from you. He was done with me. He would go on romantic weekends with other women. I think I may have been jealous to some degree. His message to me was, you want to live in my house, you get the bare minimum. You're not going to give me sex ... I'm not going to give you anything.

I don't care if anyone reads this and says, "You can't verify your father was in romantic love with you." It doesn't matter if it is true or not. He is dead. We will never know. But I can tell you what matters is I am willing to expose these dark revelations to give you courage to trust the instinctual thoughts that start to come to you as you heal. Who gives a shit if it's right or wrong? It's the lifetime of reactions that manifested we need to put an end to. Your focus is healing you into a strong, beautiful, whole realized soul. Not verifying facts for a court case. There will be no court case. We are peeling back the layers to claim who we are as our own glorious selves in perfectly aligned bodies that deserve love and sex. I am not going to let the rest of my life go by in a sad shell of what repressed inside me for four decades. Neither will you.

WRITING PROMPT:

What instinctual thoughts or revelations about the abuse can you not bear to think about or want to discount? Write them all down now. Whether you can verify them or not with your abuser, you have the right to be witnessed in these memories and understand you are far from insane.

My warped sexual desire developed into the fundamental belief that sex is the commodity for romantic love. I had no idea that the deepest core of my being was a beautiful sensual woman dying to come out and be in her fullest human expression. For decades I was verbosely sexual yet held back by the belief that because I stopped giving sex to an adult man as a young girl, I was left empty, dirty and alone.

I would sit in AA meetings and I hear women share about drinking and fucking at thirteen years old. I started younger, but not with boys my age. In fact, right as I turned thirteen I walked five miles down long farm roads in Warren, RI to get to my boyfriend's house so I could give him a blow job. I needed to initiate myself to the world of men who I could receive accolades from for my sexual skills that was not my dad.

As early as seventeen, with a powerful rage, I would scream at boyfriends who in my perception, did not fuck or love me enough.

"Get the fuck out mother fucker. You don't want to give me love? You don't want to fuck me? Fuck you," I would scream on public streets, ditching out of moving cars, running off late night in foreign cities.

I was very proud of my willingness to have sex in public places, and keeping track of a healthy sex count every week. Sex became part of the survival tactics to never slow down and face my demons. It was another additive to the lies. There was no grace, light, God or love in any of it.

WRITING PROMPT:

What has been your relationship to your sexual desire? Write about a sexual encounter where you felt trapped by history and yet couldn't pull yourself out of it.

In order to change the way I saw romantic love or a life partner/husband, I cleaned up the addictions and the shame. I then explored what felt good outside the shame. I leaned into that sexy sensual woman. What does she wear? What does she hope for from a partner to hear her, to put up with her, to love every single aspect of her deep full womanhood. Every single component. There was a part of my dad that put up with every part of me. Besides getting really mad at me for not being able to comprehend basic math, he was pretty chill about me, and even was one of my key fans in my movie making days. He came to one of my film premieres in New York and watched both shows. He loved me, but he had already had a romantic sexual relationship with the child me. I couldn't reconcile that ever in my brain when I was in denial, and while he was around, I couldn't get better.

His death eventually set me free. I couldn't even write the eulogy. I didn't know at the time why but to write about him made me feel sick.

I don't have to be an 8 year old now to cope with my new-found love for self. I can love myself as a grown woman exploring boundaries and a shame-free life. Life is so grand shame free. This stuff is pouring out of me. My dad was in love with me and I can break out of that now. You can break out of the bond of your abusive situation by knowing their love for you was not the love you deserve.

WRITING PROMPT:

What love do you feel you deserve? Write about the truest love that you, separate from your past, would enjoy experiencing on a daily basis. How does sex factor in?

I grew up serving a purpose for my dad and that dynamic of the "wife". A self-imposed purpose of service and serving in a very unhealthy way. So of course I had no idea how to be in an equal partnership where both people asked for their needs to be met in a loving equal fashion of doing service to the love that they fostered between them. My dad had a hot and cold personality (which later I self-diagnosed as untreated bi-polar), so when I dated men who had uneven personalities, I thought as long as I served my purpose of showing up, I was being "good." To come in alignment with true love, "good" is the lowest bar. First, in order to aspire to a mind-blowing romantic connection, I had to know exactly what I wanted from a partner, how I wanted to be treated and to not waver in my confidence.

I fell in love for the first time in my recovery from abuse and alcoholism with a man around the time I starting writing this book. I really fell for him. I thought we talked the same language because we met in SLAA, but in reality we were just bumbling around in the dark together. When he broke up with me by email, I thought it was the most devastating event in the world. I had ignored the little signs it was coming. I was new to this break up game. I was always the one breaking up with people and not too gracefully I may add. The email break up seemed cowardly, but what was worse was that he had failed me. I thought we were in this together. We had shared pain of our childhoods, of our adulthoods. He had so many pieces of what I thought I wanted. He was respectful and responsible, and he told me I was beautiful. He was fun and we had good sex. But it burned and fizzled too hard and too fast for both of us. We were not healthy enough to have an adult relationship. Both of us saw the red flags and thought it was a parade. I had lost myself in his problems, drama and delaying this beautiful journey with me that I needed to have. The experience knocked me on my ass with men. I talked to a few women friends about it and decided to make myself accountable with them. I took a full year off of all men and decided to fall in love with me. To fall in love with me was one of the hardest challenges I have ever faced and one of the best decisions I have ever made.

It was scary to see how I had filled myself so much with the obsession of a man wanting and needing me like the relationship with my dad played out so many times in the incest in my childhood, and also in some kind of unsaid twisted co-dependence in my adult relationship with him. When I was celibate, everything changed. The constant stream of analysis and fear with male partners went away and I was able to truly see my life path and connect with God, my life callings and my sobriety differently than ever before. What was so cool about this time in my life, a very precious time, as lonely as it could be, was I have it now to hold onto to give me strength. I can always make it on my own two feet. It's not that scary. Bringing in a romantic relationship adds value to my life; it is not THE value. When I struggle with my will in a time line with a man, or in fear it won't last, I can reign those obsessions in and give the time clock to God. No man needs to be beaten with a bat.

WRITING PROMPT:

Have you ever taken time to be celibate before? If you are currently not sexual, or have not been for a long while, write about the relationship you have with your body right now. How do you celebrate all its inner workings, curves and strengths?

Finally after the year off, I started dating. I had never dated but I had to learn about men as people, and all kinds and types. I had choices instead of just going with who picked me, or who I had sex with. I was faced with new big girl stuff that I had not really dealt with in marriages and also in my serial monogamy. Like STD tests and birth control options. It was my responsibility to take care of my body and allow a man into my full life. Celibacy had given me the gift of perspective that men were human just like me trying to do the best they could to be loved. I started to no longer see them as loathsome creatures out to make my life miserable when they didn't do what I wanted. Or didn't tell me they loved me, or talked continuously about their ex wives. I realized the most painful part of accepting my divorce from my children's dad was sure, he didn't really love me deeply in a romantic sense, but how could he? I was a rageful, untreated alcoholic hiding the secret of sexual abuse. We came together to make our beautiful children, and align some kind of soul contract, but it was painful to spend a decade with someone who didn't love me in the way I knew somewhere deep down in my unconscious I deserved one day.

You can decide facts of your past will no longer trap you in their dark secrets. You don't need to beat anyone up anymore. We are warriors who go into battle and come out ready for peace. Are you ready for peace? Can you start to date people peacefully? It was rough going at first but God gave me some good candidates as practice dates. I wrestled the dragon inside me that wanted to hook into an addictive relationship with an unavailable man like my father. Instead I knew I wanted to go on nice dates with men who didn't need to dry hump me in the car. Then one day, should any date progress to a relationship, on the front of sexuality, I could decide maybe, maybe not. I was vigilantly watchful of old patterns and checked in with women friends before dates.

WRITING PROMPT:

Have you dated while you are in recovery? Even if you are married, do you go on dates with your partner? How about dates with yourself? Write about one of your favorite dates and why.

My curiosity had to come into play with men versus just lock down the one that shows interest in me and then be resentful most of the time he is not the right match for me. If he would just change ... if I would just be different. I enjoyed meeting men that could make me laugh, be gracious, and the best part was, after a couple dates I had I didn't have to tell them about my trauma of sexual abuse ... they didn't know anything but that I didn't drink, or I had been married a couple times. Then if we didn't totally gel, we moved on.

I urge you to be curious in all areas of your life including this one, but take it slow. How wonderful to fall in love with someone in a curious way!

WRITING PROMPT:

Have you made a list of how you want to be loved by a partner without judgment or analysis of your needs? Then ask yourself if you are willing to do all those actions you are asking that person to do. If not, then look at where you can better build character before you expect a romantic partner to fill that void.

Due to the severe trust issues stemming from the abuse, I wasn't fully able to love a partner without losing my identity and blaming them for absorbing me. The truth is I want to know how to love someone in a spiritual, emotional and physical relationship unconditionally where we don't need anything from each other besides love, connection and companionship.

I completely respect those of you in recovery from sexual abuse with no desire for male or female romantic relationships because of the struggle with feeling safe. To struggle is exhausting and takes the joy out of romantic love. We want to get out of the struggle and into the part that brings us the fulfillment we deserve from romantic love. If you want to explore, in the beginning have a lot of support and love of other women, spirituality and a fundamental platform of self that is founded on your inherent good no matter what and you can STOP seeing someone if it is causing you too many sleepless nights or despair. You can say in a loving way, "I'm sorry. I need a break. This is painful for me and I would like to revisit this when I have some peace."

You couldn't easily walk away from the abuse but you can walk away from a bad romantic relationship when you have build the survivor power of your core self.

WRITING PROMPT:

What relationships have you stayed in too long, even when you intuitively knew they treated you in questionable ways? Or you treated them poorly?

I have to admit, it was kind of fun to have frustrating dating experiences other attractive smart "normal" women had. I felt normal! One classic is the disappearance of the guy after date four. It happened to me both times after any conversation about sexuality or intimacy. They just bailed. They saw I wasn't going to be fun sex girl on date five. I was asserting my abstinence with men I thought had potential. Still they were far from my worthy values! I would ignore big red flags like swearing too much, drinking too much or clearly harboring resentments about a cheating ex! Regardless, these men were practice ground, and I did them no harm. We often had fun until the fun was done. What I was able to do with these men was hold a space for me to be completely and absolutely my full self. I didn't feel besides wanting to show up looking pretty and positive for our dates that I had to be anything than what I was. A divorced mom with two children who has lots of history and stories, and discovering what I like in all areas. I think God does for me right now what I cannot do for myself. My friend, an Akashic record reader, told me that I don't need to be in charge of my love life. That the serendipities had it handled. I just needed to wear lipstick and show up.

WRITING PROMPT:

Who do you think is in charge of you falling in love, or your dating plan? Do you have a coach, a support circle? Do you allow spirituality to come into play when seeking a mate?

Sometimes I would have dark chains of thought. I'd feel exploited, destroyed and think that a man is a monster or I've somehow either made a mess of a relationship with a man, or worse, gotten sucked into some royal mess. I would feel desperate to get out like a rat in a cage. They wrap around me and spiral and I get lost in their chalky hue, wanting to erase what I feel in euphoric present. Then I realize despite my non-productive thinking, I am receiving valuable information about the course of my life. It could very well be a subtle warning, or a whisper from God. My dad's shadow and ownership of my trusting little girl was inserted into all my relationships and I get to weed him away, blade by emotional blade. He breached my trust in childhood, abandoned me and took away an incestuous love. He warped all areas of my life including money and sex by not being honest about either.

I gave my power away to men and attracted people (and not just romantically) that liked my damage. The "we are broken together" philosophy is a pile of crap. Align with healthy people, and you will heal. Be very vigilant about this practice. Sure, help a friend in need, but keep your soul aligned with your brighter light.

In romantic love, what is that fine line of being "abused" or "used" as a woman recovering from sexual abuse? When do you know it feels right? Only you can allow yourself to be abused now. As a child, we had no choices with abuse. Now you do but do you make them as a victim or a courageous survivor with smarts and confidence.

I didn't understand men. I thought they were all predators and sometimes I caved into it. I did not start to see men compassionately as human beings until a few years into my sexual abuse recovery, a full year off any sex or men, and dating.

Just like an alcoholic changes from beer to wine, or drinks only in the evening, I thought maybe if I branch out and date other ethnicities I won't have the same problems. It must be white men, I thought. Still, I attracted people with an apparent dark side. The darkness and inconsistency of my father's love still energetically drew people in. I made a commitment right to date nice men and to get some help. I enlisted the help of my beautiful client RaShawn Renee. Recovered from a history of physical and mental abuse in her past romantic relationship, she helped me to communicate my worth and value with my current boyfriend from the get go, and set expectations. I could say "That is not pleasing for me," without condemning him with a judge or jury, or rage. I highly recommend not just any dating coach as you navigate romantic love as a survivor, but someone who also relates to your history, and has entered into their own successful, powerful romantic relationship.

There will always be lessons to learn, especially if you stretch your neck out. Many people would be impressed with how committed I was to dating every week no matter what my workload or kid schedule. I knew how valuable the lessons were for me with men, trust and myself with dating. I fell for a guy on a dating site that split his time between LA and Boston, but he was really never here. Instead, since he was so unhappy being alone after the end of a 25 year marriage, he would keep me talking on Skype until almost 2 or 3 am his time, which is also way past my bedtime. He would tell me how lovely I was, the way I moved. He played me music and videos and I was so hooked. I plunged into great fantasy about our future together. I finally disentangled myself from the situation when he came to dinner here in LA and wanted me to give him a hand job in his car on the public street in Brentwood. I thought, Kim, what are you doing with this lonely idiot? I told him no, and went home. I wanted to blame him for being so sick, but I had to look at the fact that I had attracted him and signed up for really poor treatment and no respect.

I decided maybe it was time to really focus only on men with all the qualities of my vision, and if I wanted sex, I could find a booty call. At forty-six years old, it can be pretty fun to have a twenty-six year old booty call but if you are really looking for love, it stops being fun after the first time and you are back where you started. Wanting a deep meaningful connection.

WRITING PROMPT:

Can you bring distinction to "hook ups" versus commitments? Write freely what a torrid sexual affair as a booty call would look like. Lay it out and sit in it. What comes up for you as possible and impossible in that situation? Are you allowed to have your sexual needs met in a primal manner?

Now I am in the new position where I don't want to manage love, or be forced to do love. I am readying myself for love. Am I completely healed and whole? No, but I have an idea from all the trials during recovery how I want to love in my beautiful self. You too will find a middle ground that is empowering, vulnerable and scary at the same stroke. One day I was praying to God to understand how I reveal the story of sexual abuse to any new guy I date. Not trauma bonding, but letting him know just so he can know me. Just like he would reveal some trauma he had in his life. The answer I received was, does it matter? It may be an integral part of my life, and my mission to help other people heal, but is it really part of our dialogue? That was not the case when I started to face sexual abuse. I had to tell everyone. Now I see I need to simply walk in a stronger sense of self and that story is a truth but it is not shackling me or preventing me from loving all the parts that have made me who I am today.

In the past, I thought my purpose was to fall in love with a man because I was seeking what that felt like. I didn't trust that I would know. It was so far from my scope of belief. It still is in a lot of ways because I think I'm falling in love with people who I then never see after the fourth date! The key is to slow down and not let the sexual override the emotional. If sex is a dominant part of your operating system, then vigilance is key. You will be up to your old tricks. I stuck to very clear values and "rules" to call in my future husband. The man who gets to spend the most amazing decades of my life with me. The one I have been growing and developing to call in.

WRITING PROMPT:

What are your dating rules and values? Be honest, are you looking for a partner for life or are you looking to simply have fun? There is nothing wrong with sex and fun, as long as you are safe, and do not breach your core values.

In dating, or even my current relationship, if you don't call me in advance to schedule time with me, even if I am home plucking eyebrow hairs, I'm not available. Sure, I can be and am very spontaneous, but I am setting up a respectability factor that my time is precious. If you want to romance me, you need to have put some thought into it. Once you have sex, you suddenly want this great respect and all these rules. The rules of the direction of the relationship have to be talked about before hand. Men like to know the woman has value for herself. I met a man and I made it clear I was not a booty call. We hung out once a month, but since we were not sleeping together, I didn't have a lot of rules besides treat me nice, adore me, be interesting and stay honest. Then he tried to pressure me to have sex and wasn't open to a relationship discussion. See ya! Kissing even affects your framework because it the pheromones all ignited. Do not discount the attaching power of those hormones! So I have to tell myself I can control my behavior and continue to get to know this person before I give it away.

As painful as all this was, through all the lessons with dating, I was still falling in love with myself and the best antidote to losing my cool was staying out of any kind of romantic fantasy. I had to stick to the facts. I met a funny woman on a plane who told me she went on 120 sober dates with men to get to know men as people, and to change her perceptions of the man she was looking for. She met her husband of now thirteen years on the 120th date, and he was short and bald. Not at all what she thought she would meet. The interesting shift for me with dating was no matter who I met, I was able to get up the next day and be present for all my responsibilities and desires. There were of course the great breakdowns every time I thought I was falling in love with someone, but I see now it was just a cleansing of the old patterns. "I think I am falling in love with someone," after three dates is a big red flag for me. The feelings inside may be legitimate but as my adult woman took over the lonely teenage girl who had messy young relationships, I could divert the energy back to reality. You must be vigilant about sticking with who you are today in romantic love.

You don't need to force any connections. If destined, they develop with openness and trust in the person who earns it. If it feels heavy pulling the "right one" towards you, stop struggling, have fun and continue exploring with an open heart.

WRITING PROMPT:

What do you believe men you date see first in you? Write about your first impression so when you walk out that door and share yourself with another in the process of looking for a partnership you can carry that clarity.

At a certain point I didn't want to go to my SLAA meetings and stare at the same "losers" talking about their inability to cope with sex and love. I didn't want to be reminded I hadn't cracked the code yet either and here we were on a Friday afternoon completely dysfunctional in a circle in some church whining while the rest of the world did productive things like got a job so they could be self supporting or did yoga or planned a fun family weekend getaway. I let that anger surface because it showed me how badly I wanted to be well. I sat in those uncomfortable spaces and continued in SLAA because leaving was not a decision of ease and good. I was still fighting it. When I started dating more, I learned I was actually safe in my behavior, even if I made mistakes like sleeping with someone too soon. I was no longer interested in sex texting sprees for false highs. It's just flat out a waste of time. That is a far leap from the woman four years ago who used to sit in her kitchen stoned and drinking wine while her kids watched TV and madly sex text with a man twenty years older in such a desperate longing aroused way. Now you try and send me a dick pic and my immediate response is "What the fuck is wrong with you?" and BLOCKED.

While the SLAA program was crucial as a side bar during the first two years of my abuse recovery, it started to feel a bit shaming. So I left. It is not a choice for everyone. It just felt right for me as a sexual abuse survivor. People came into my life right after that decision that had smart advice about dating and also about opening your heart. So the journey continued on yet another spiritual teaching level that all leads to more self-love.

Both my marriages clearly suffered because of my repression of my sexual abuse secret. While not sharing this information on date four or even month six is not imperative, before you marry someone, I highly suggest that you do get this information on the table. If the love foundation is as strong as you hope, this information will not change the love you built. Your recovery is the cornerstone to which you can freely love as an adult woman. It doesn't have to be diminished by trauma tales. It can be diminished by secrets. Men healing are not my project. For a while men were attracted to me to heal them in some way from the endings of their long repressed marriages they finally got out of. That is not my role, but I can also be aware they are in some way healing me. In romantic partnership, we heal with each other and grow. It doesn't come from trauma bonding, but honor and value. The secrets will be revealed slowly in God's time if the relationship has the legs to go the distance.

WRITING PROMPT:

When in the relationship or dating process with a man, do you feel compelled to trauma bond over your abuse? What do you feel if you don't share? Like you are keeping a secret?

When we were abused we may have liked it, in my case, it felt good to be touched because it was the only parental touch I had. I was too young to know it was destroying my young heart and altering my perceptions for healthy adulthood.

I have talked in this book about splitting and disassociation in a very radical, long lasting way. In other abuse books, it is talked about it as a prolonged state we must endure. For me, I have melded my two sides into one complete whole. Once there were two sides of Kim dueling each other. Now anxiety attacks warn me I'm splitting away from the present moment and my core self. I cannot fully embrace love of self or another without taking good care of myself, which means one thought at a time. I make a daily choice to align with the really joyous euphoric me, high on spirituality and life and faith, and turn away from the dark me.

Sounds plays a big factor in my romantic tolerance. I learned this when I was single and coping with the meowing of our cat. He is a doll. A rescue who just really is so peaceful and loving but occasionally out of boredom or smelling other cats outside, he howls. If I am working at home, it cuts to my core. How dare he just howl around my house and have a voice that says what he wants? I would lunge at him to scare him off if he was meowing in my room, or yell "Shut up!" I would laugh thinking what the neighbors must think of this crazy woman yelling at her poor house cat. My male cat became a project assigned by my Alanon sponsor to be like a spouse. When his howling would drive me nuts, she'd say, "You can't just scream at your spouse, especially if you love him." My male cat was my training ground for healthy co-habitation with a man. So instead of shouting at him in annoyance, I'd be gentle, or if he was annoying, or I felt taxed, I would leave.

I had to work through the cat sounds reminding me of that young primal inner child that was abused and no one listened. That cried for love when there was operative pain with the urethra. The child that was forced down and silenced. Shut up, shut up I hissed. I could feel my anger towards the cat coursing through my veins and I would grab him and hold him down really hard. I was now the abuser and he can't talk back to me or get away. As the cat breathed under my firm hand, I had enough self-awareness to see these are the remaining predatorial feelings of my retaliation for what had been done to me. Annoyance at a cat meow was progress from throwing glasses in kitchens and smashing stereo tuners with bats. Since I am 99% of the time loving and kind to him and feed him and change his litter and play with him, he did not seem too freaked out by the seething anger that he must have felt in my hand. I gathered myself, I let go of the feeling of power that one gets when they abuse, and I stroked his fur.

"It's going to be okay," I told him, but I was really telling me.

This was not a time for isolation or alienation. I told my AA sponsor, I told my friends in recovery. I was harsh to my cat. I started to pray to God about it. I prayed more. When I rose in the morning and he meowed I bent down to stroke him. I fed him. I gave him water. When I didn't want to, I played with him. One night I had such a massive anxiety attack, he stayed with me, circled me, and as I stroked his fur, the anxiety in my chest lessoned. Like a partner who you show not just the perfect glossy you, but the messy you and they stick around. Sure, sometimes the cat still bugs me. But I don't hurt him. In fact, I hurt myself. He was meowing at me in the tub the other day and I shooed him more violently with my arm than is necessary and in the process slammed the soft part of my arm onto the metal lip of the shower door, causing an insanely huge bruise all down my arm. I realized, Wow, I am really harming myself when I am mean. It's simply emotional immaturity. I can still be an angry child. This journey does not have a graduation date, but we develop smarter skills. I knew I had to be vigilant about my young unbridled anger rearing up in a romantic partnership. The man who bonds with me could be a target of sporadic aggression and my job is to protect him by loving me first. I have God with me all the time. I have God, my higher power, in my mind and heart wherever I go. I am safe. You are safe. You are good.

WRITING PROMPT:

Can you "practice" healthy relationships of love? Animals, children, friends. People who challenge you...

An angry child is an unfit persona for a healthy adult romantic relationship! Anger needs to be recalibrated to be less potent and disconnected to old shame. People evoke my anger and I can say that out loud and not feel shame about it. I am not ashamed to say what I feel anymore because typically I have thought it out, prayed on it, written about it and decided how it would help a situation versus destroy it because I want to feel safe. Mean what you say but don't say it mean is a HUGE slogan for abuse survivors because we want so much to pillage and destroy every hapless soul who doesn't understand why we are so angry!!!

The ultimate project is falling into self-love. You will know how to fall in love romantically when you are completely one with you. You don't need to control love to know what it is. Like that foreigner song, *I want to know what love is. I want you to show me.* I've been asking men to show me and they have failed me. Love happens between two healthy people. It is a childish dream to have a man be the one to lead you to love. We are all stumbling around in the dark doing the best we can. As long as I stay curious and don't hurt myself and others, I can love for love. I can have sex for fun. I can have sex with love. And I can love sex.

WRITING PROMPT:

I want you to make a list of all the words you use in your mind to describe the act of sex in romantic love. Then ask for sex in all the ways you feel represent who you are … observe all the sexual sides of you and when you are done, thank yourself for having so many perspectives to sort through and understand.

I had a breakthrough when I heard from a few strong women from abusive pasts that I had to be really ready to fall in love. I had to be available. It struck me that I had never been available. My relationship coach/client/friend RaShawn asked me one day if I was ready to get married? I hesitated.

"You are not ready," she said. "When you don't hesitate, we will know you are ready."

I thought on that. I had claimed I was ready, but maybe I really wasn't. For a couple weeks, I tried on not being ready. I slept with this guy and dated this guy. Then again, I asked myself, and saw I was ready. I had to own it though, and operate in a way that let my future husband know I was for keeps. This was for real. I started to say I was looking for a husband, and it slowly became the truth.

While finishing this book, I met an amazing, kind and generous man. My heart blew open in ways I was not aware were possible. All the work I had done on myself and all the trials and tribulations of getting to know men not just as abusers, but as people, culminated in our meeting. I have felt emotions that are steeped in profound gratitude in the way we move through time together. Two adults who took this long to find each other, and have been refining ourselves the whole way. Like a readying for this very moment in time. For him to love me as deeply as he does, my self-love is always paramount. I need to love me first always. All the loves since recovery have been gifts to me, teaching me about male-female love, and I am so grateful I didn't shut the door to any of them. I learned the fundamentals of how to be a good romantic partner by being a good partner to myself. As a healer said to me recently while releasing trauma from my body, "Kim, you have had so much trauma in your life. You are ready for a lifetime of joy."

I believe that!!!

Do you believe that?

CHAPTER NINETEEN
RELEASED

On Father's day 2016, my dad released a bit of his hold on me. It was at an open eye meditation. As my teacher and I connected our energies in that powerful space, I recall the feeling as it came through me. I felt my dad's spirit was finally healed. I felt that he was giving me the message that he now could send good and light to me. As I sat in the meditation I thought, have I finally done the deep work to release myself from that abusive relationship? My father's spirit healing in Heaven soothed me in my heart on that meditative day. Releasing my dad's soul disentangles mine. My vision, my feeling in this meditation, was forgiveness based on my own father's spirit forgiving himself. He loathed himself and each time he abused me, he instilled into me that self-loathing. He reached out in this meditation with an attempt to be a father who would guide a daughter to love herself on this earth, and be a strong confident woman. Go learn how to be treated, I release you, the voice said. I don't need to say "yes" when I mean "no". And I don't need to feel bad about choice.

The following weekend, as I watched my two young daughters and their friend run with a hand made kite down a hill, I thought, how free they are to not be obsessed with a man, men, partners, love. They are free to think of themselves as shaping units, their imaginations, their solitary times reading, playing, exploring – they may not understand their range of emotions but at least they have them all to themselves, not hinged on this guy or that guy or this hook for sexual satisfaction to be the one for someone. I thought how precious that time in life is to see them living like this. While on a wonderful paddle boating experience with these children in the warm summer sun, under the spray of the projectile fountain, I saw how I think a man knowing of my existence completes me. I grew sad at that moment that it couldn't just be good enough for me to know about me. I yearned for my own innocent childhood devoid of the abuse. I'd always been hooked on my dad who made my existence all through childhood attached to his attention or lack thereof. These epiphanies would not have come had I not been pushing through boundaries and insisting on having fun with me, and my children, or friends. Not just in a romantic paradigm. My idea of going out, seeing the arts, exploring, being seen just as me as a unit all to herself.

As they ran with the kite I smiled, I took video. I was so happy their lives are not filled with abuse. It made me feel hope.

The next week I stretched my comfort zone again. I took the new Expo line from Culver City to Santa Monica to free concerts on the Santa Monica pier. I felt actually guilty about going and doing this. Like I was reckless and irresponsible. That voice that says "Who are you to actually have fun as a human being just because, by yourself?" I ignored the mental chatter and boarded the train. How had my life gotten so small? I used to travel all over the world by myself without fear -Australia, and Cuba, take subways all over New York. Make films in Oregon…but I had booze, and sex addiction, and secrets and the cloak of "working for something professionally" to encircle me. Now I was sober, and with myself and satisfied with a good day's work, and taking the train to Santa Monica felt like a big adventure! I realized to get sober, and to heal from trauma, you have to close in the circle of your life first as you release so much pain and emotion. Then in time, you can stretch that circle out. I sat on the train and thought wow, life is going to get big for me again. Can I walk into the world knowing there is good and there is bad? All my prior adventures are not for naught. They shaped me to be the full visionary I can be today to hold space for other's visions. I don't even need to give the facts of my credentials. I just need to hold the space. My concern now wasn't having fun, it was opening my net and my world to meet people for all sorts of reasons … I saw that the lines could blur, but all the parts had to be there. That was a lot of surrender. A total free fall.

WRITING PROMPT:

Where can you go today that can release you a bit more? Where have you not given yourself permission to go alone?

I found out that while my dad had released me in that meditation, I had not forgiven my dad. I had not gotten honest about how I really felt about him. Sure I had gone through justification process of his own personal abuse history, but I wasn't truly owning it the forgiveness.

This book laid dormant during this time. The last two chapters not complete. I couldn't pick it up. I knew that very new feelings were starting to emerge for me with the meditation, connection with my clients' stories, my relationship with my children and dating. Through living a bigger life in sobriety and spirituality, I was learning about the abuse, my recovery and my heart opening more to love and letting the past leave me. I was only to be in Self and really not pay any heed anymore to all the opinions in my head that were based on only what I had experienced in the past. If I was to rewrite my life in a new vision that was bolder and bigger, I had to tune in to what God had in store for me, and I knew it was a hell of a lot better than what I had experienced in the past.

"My father did me a favor by dying," I said one day point blank to a friend.

They paused. "I'm speechless," he said. "And that is rare."

"I'm sorry," I said, "But it is the truth, and not in a cruel way."

"I can hear that," he said. "In the way you spoke."

WRITING PROMPT:

Where have you felt fully candid and realized about how you speak of our abuser? What has that opened up or shut down for you after?

It was true and I had to work for about a day after to not go into shame and fear about the truth of that statement. I felt pulled to still sympathize, and hedge, well, maybe that was a little harsh or hard. But it wasn't. My dad was an alcoholic who slowly killed himself, and was my abuser. He had to die. His suffering was too great. There was no other recourse.

I went to a women's AA retreat where there was a profound breathing workshop for trauma. The facilitator asked us to set an intention on our mats in a room all together and I set mine to release my dad from my love life and to no longer have him be a part of my DNA. I said to him, I know you are dead but now it is time to really put you to rest. I made the assertion he can no longer have power over me anymore, a power that evoked a life time of rage at my primary male role model not treating me with kindness, safety and reverence as a father should. When I was a little girl, his foul moods were scary. Then he was affectionate. He had been my lover in a sick dark place. I won't have it anymore. No longer does my inner child have to cope with a daddy who loves her one minute and is cruel and mean the next. There is no light in the darkest of those shadows. It just has to be brightened. I won't live in the cold dampness anymore. I was born unto him, I have his spunk, charisma, sexuality, intelligence but I no longer will apply the patterns to the romantic experiences I long to have.

When the practitioner started the music, I started to sob. She said this would happen. The deep belly chest mouth breath causes your hands to lose feeling and your brain to be numb and you just feel this deep release and sadness. I know that I got rid of him, so much of him in that session. My chest got damp and my vagina was wet (yet not wet, just the sensation in my pants). I want to know and understand a man as Kim, not as Kim who has the warped patterns and imprinting of her dad and incest. It's interesting but I once said to a guy, I like when you say my name "Kim". It grounded me at that time as who I am as a woman today. I walked away exhausted from the exercise but I knew I was sane, whole and complete. My dad was gone.

Releasing my dad also releases my witnessing how he always struggled with money. He was a smart lawyer and he would have impulses to jump on a business deal or open his own firm, but he had no belief in himself to do any day by day follow through. No one probably believed in him either. He would give me some money, a few hundred bucks here and there, when I was a struggling young adult but he had already imprinted on me by abusing me that my identity was connected to his. So I took on the belief that I would always under-earn and experience financial tragedy.

Releasing my dad's hold on me opened me up to see that I could break the pattern of not having financial abundance. I started to invest money directly into my own personal development. I took a course on money and saw holes in where I thought I had control over money, but then would fearfully overspend or go into scarcity. It was the same emotional pendulum that would swing in all areas of my life from the abuse. Black or white. Fucked or abandoned.

WRITING PROMPT:

What is your current relationship with money? Did the abuser buy you gifts or alcohol or pay your way? Or was it the opposite where you were abused and deprived. Write about how you invest in yourself and your happiness today.

Financial fear has to be released in order to fully explore all your survivor power and go after the life you want to live. We need money to provide for our families, build businesses, give to charities and see the world. Loathsome body images and depravity of the beautiful special little gifts of life has to be released. Screaming at people has to be released. Beating yourself up for not being enough, knowing enough, doing enough, has to be released.

In order to take care of your whole soul, abuse has to be released from every single area of your life because they were all touched. You are no longer a slave to your circumstances. You have been set free by you!

It's time to kick abuse in the ass, and by doing so, you assume you need to get into every corner and cranny until there no longer exists not even a vapor of its power.

WRITING PROMPT:

How does the concept of "kicking abuse in the ass" sit with you? Does it bring up defensive thinking or does it make you feel happy? Put your self in the boxing ring with abuse and see what happens.

I have to release that I don't currently engage my mom in the stories or facts of the abuse. I told her today by text that I had finished my book. I give her a lot of credit for not saying "Am I in it? What will the relatives on the East Coast say?" No instead she texted back a heart and said, you have courage. My mom had no idea I was free falling. I release my mom having to shoulder any more of my burden today. I want to love her and hold her. She is going to be seventy years old. It's time to love. To care. To laugh and to grow. It is vast.

WRITING PROMPT:

Go to the store and buy the prettiest card you can find. Hell, spend the five dollars that nice cards cost these days. Write yourself a thank you note for reading this book, doing the writing exercises, taking time to get to know you better and want to be in the world. Then write out what you release. Mail the letter to yourself.

When you get the letter in the mail, after you read it, write how you feel.

CHAPTER TWENTY
NO MORE LIES

I told myself one big long cruel lie for forty-four years. I lied while the abuse was happening by omission, and I lied after it in denial. I buried the lie as deeply as one can into the recesses of my mind. The lie may have killed me if I hadn't seen with spirituality, sobriety and God that I had a shot at a real true honest full life. We have the capacity to be tremendous liars to protect ourselves and not get vulnerable, but we need to be honest. It's not a protection at all to lie. It's a constant rejection of our honest selves.

Taking my life back was what I thought I was doing at one point in recovery, but the truth was, I was no longer lying to myself. I wasn't fantasizing about some false life that was less than what I deserved. I wasn't evading true love of self to protect myself. I was not lying about the capacity I now had to create all the life I wanted to fully live. I was in charge. I had all the power. I did not need to give it away. Part of that work involved not just changing my old thinking but being honest about how happy I wanted to be. I chose to find an existence that was filled with a mindset of peace and prosperity. I stopped fighting the fight. I experienced life in an affirming abundant giving way.

I still have the capacity to want to protect myself. It is not a horrible trait. We can be warriors and savvy people out there in the world. Protecting yourself against others who are safe and want to love you though can be a problem. I also can feel caged in when I don't have enough space, and create false stories in my head about my reality. Sometimes that is simply my alcoholism that wants to get me isolated and alone so I will escape with substances. Whatever your go to is for escape, you don't need to be hiding and alone anymore with your abuse. I hear you. We all hear you. You are no longer alone. We can make ourselves separate or part of. Whatever your personality allows you to be out in the world, know your desires and dreams make you very unique.

There are basic principles I adhere to when I wake. I need to practice affirmations about abundance and say prayers, often both. I follow my gratitude with an open eye meditation practice. I eat breakfast and have coffee. I embrace my children no matter what time they awake, some days not so easy when I am wound up about something. I learn how to breathe through anxiety attacks and I am not ashamed of them. They key in my life when I show up for my business, my kids, my life partner, my friends, is to be fully 100% present and be okay with all the feelings in my mind and body that come along for the ride. Taking my body back means I can be with others because they are not going to abuse me. Even if you talk to me in a way I don't like, or have an opinion I don't agree with, you are not my dad causing me to lie there while you defile me. You just are not. We need to trust people again and join the energies of love in the world so we can bring the power of who we are as survivors out into the global space.

You are not bad. I am not bad. I was never a bad girl because I was abused. I deserve all the same benefits and considerations as any other human on this planet. I am no longer a half human. I don't carry any more secrets. I live a very sane and honorable life. You can too. You will and it will all be okay.

What I pray for in all of us is enough healing so we can have the empathy and compassion for men and women who still live trapped inside their old story that they can't have any love besides that primal initial love of their sexual abuser. It is so hard to break that old story. We can help them by example of our journey.

We can kick abuse in the ass.

"You say to this person, I can't see you anymore.
I need a happy place.
A place where I can be like a fast flowing stream."

ACKNOWLEDGEMENTS

I would not have been the pillar of strength required to finish this book without the love, kindness and support of my friends Stephanie Zhong and Nancy Manpearl. They were quick to remind me when my old thinking, denial and limiting beliefs were in charge, and to love on myself.

Nicole Criona gave editorial notes on the rough draft of the book, suggesting I expand the writing exercises, and infusing me with the confidence to keep forging forward.

At completion, I needed a first reader for the book; a terrifying endeavor after it was just my story for so long. I am forever grateful to Joshua Howard for spending an entire weekend reading and telling me about all the parts he loved that made him weep. He is a blessing and a gift of the beautiful life I have today.

I am forever grateful to God for showing me daily miracles, and one of them being the right path to my publisher Waterside Press through the shelves of Barnes and Noble, and a cold call to Claudia Riemer Boutote.

I am forever grateful to my attorney Jamice Oxley for fielding my calls with calm collected grace in the process of releasing this book.

I am forever grateful to my book clients, and how their vulnerability and transparency as writers provided to me the fortitude to soldier on.

I am forever grateful to my therapist Rena K. When she agreed to work with me, she took on a lifetime of denial, sadness and anger. I can't express enough how she taught me what it felt like to be truly loved without any judgment.

If Kelly Morgan hadn't run one of the most amazing Artist's Way courses, I don't know if this book would exist. In that circle, week after week, I re-discovered my own artist way.

Cover artist Rick Penn-Kraus went above and beyond for the cover art of the book. He brought decades of publishing house experience to the table, not just in the design, but helping me hash out the title. I couldn't have wished for a better collaboration at this crucial time.

Finally, I acknowledge Jim A. for being my wingman when I finally told my mom about the abuse, and Britton D. for holding space for my raw tender self in the first year of recovery.

Someday my children will read this book. I will have talked with them about it before hand. I want to thank them in advance for giving me the opportunity through their childhoods to play, laugh and live mine once again. A long lineage of abuse stopped at me, and that alone is my greatest life victory.

About Kim O'hara

As an Intuitive Book Coach with her company, A Story Inside, Kim coaches authors through the writing of their memoirs. While the work with her clients has the goal of a finished manuscript, she is particularly focused on their journey of healing through writing. She witnesses her authors' past stories and encourages them to write new ones.

Two decades as a movie producer and screenwriter in Hollywood taught her the art of story development and artistic collaboration. Her movies starred notable actors, and screened all over the world. A few can be rented on Netflix. She trained as a writer at Stanford Writers Lab, San Jose State English Department and UCLA Advanced Screenwriter's Lab. She explored acting at the IO West Improv Intensive, but was almost kicked out for "writing everyone's parts in her head."

Kim holds A Story Inside monthly workshops where participants write through prompts to reveal their inner most fears, desires, pain and joy. In a mere day, she helps women heal through their words, unlock hidden potential, and surmount their blocks.

Her long-awaited journey through her story of sexual abuse is what really qualifies her to write this book. With an open heart, she speaks at conferences, sharing the message of writing your way through any trauma to have the life you can love.

She lives in Los Angeles, CA with her two beautiful daughters, one cat and an endless barrage of fleas.

Made in the USA
San Bernardino, CA
16 March 2018